MW01254679

Preface

THERE IS A Healing Presence within you which heals all manner of disease. To use this Healing Presence requires knowledge of God and the way He works.

Spiritual healing refers to wholeness, completeness, and perfection.

Science means knowledge of laws and principles; it means systematized and coordinated knowledge.

Knowledge of this Healing Principle is taken directly from the Bible. The means by which we unlock the mysteries and reveal the hidden meaning of the Bible from Genesis to Revelation is the science of symbology and the science of the Hebrew alphabet.

The Bible deals with spiritual and mental laws. It recognizes the fact that many of the characters, such as Jesus, Moses, Elijah, Paul, and others were real men who lived on earth; nevertheless, they also represent states of mind within all of us. The Bible is a spiritual and psychological textbook.

Through the study and application of mental laws, *you* can find the way to health, harmony, peace, and prosperity; scientific prayer is the practice of the Presence of God.

THREE STEPS IN HEALING

The first step: Think of God as the only Presence and the only Power; God is a universal, creative Spirit present everywhere—the Living Spirit Almighty fixed in your own heart. Dwell on some of the things you know to be true about God; say quietly, for example: "He is Infinite Intelligence, Absolute Goodness, Infinite Power, Indescribable Beauty, Boundless Love, Infinite Wisdom, and All-Powerful.

The second step: Forgive everyone; send loving thoughts to the whole world. Say, "I fully and freely forgive *everyone* now, and I go free."

5

Add sincerely from your heart, "I mean this, it is true." You do not have any mental reservations.

The third step: Claim calmly and lovingly that the Infinite Healing Presence of God within you is now healing your body, making it whole, pure, and perfect. Declare to yourself, "I believe this. I accept it. I know the healing is taking place now." Give thanks for the harmony and peace that are yours.

"God in the midst of you is mighty to heal."

PRACTICE OF THE PRESENCE OF GOD

THE OMNIPRESENCE OF God means that God is present at every moment of time and every point of space. To practice the Presence of God all day long is the key to harmony, health, peace, joy, and a fullness of life. Begin now to see God in everyone and in everything.

THREE STEPS IN PRACTICING THE PRESENCE

The first step: Accept the fact that God is the only Presence and the only Power. He is the very Life and Reality of you.

The second step: Realize the Presence of God in all of the members of your family and in every person you meet. Salute the Divinity from this moment forward in everyone who crosses your path.

The third step: Realize, know, and claim that everything you are and everything you see, whether it is a tree, dog, or cat, is a part of God's expression; this is the greatest thing you can do; it is powerful beyond words.

Sit down quietly two or three times a day, and think along these lines: God is all there is. He is all in all. Begin to realize that the Divine Presence is within you and within everyone around you. *"Seek, and ye shall find. Seek ye first the Kingdom of God, and his righteousness; and all these things shall be added unto you."*

CHANGE FEAR TO FAITH

WHENEVER FEAR enters your mind, it is a signal for action; do something about it immediately; never surrender to your fear. Your fear is really a desire for something better; it is a longing for freedom and peace of mind. Where will you get your freedom and peace of mind? You will find it in the thoughts of peace, freedom, and poise.

If a man loses his way in the woods at night, fear seizes him; but knowing that God is all-wise and knows the way out, he changes from fear to faith. He is now changing from the mood of fear to the mood of confidence and peace in the only Presence and the only Power. He has changed his mental attitude; this is often referred to as the Angel of God's Presence which leads him out into safety. The man who is lost turns to God in prayer and recognition, and says to himself quietly and lovingly, "God is guiding me now. He is a lamp unto my feet." He trusts and believes in this inner Light; this is the Light that lighteth every man that cometh into the world.

One with God is a majority! There is only fear and love. Fear is love in reverse. Love frees; it gives; it is the Spirit of God. Love builds the body. Love is also an emotional attachment. So fall in love with peace, gentleness, success, goodwill, and harmony, for this form of love casts out fear.

"God is love; and he that dwelleth in love dwelleth in God, and God in him."

THREE STEPS IN BANISHING FEAR

The first step: "The Lord is my light and my salvation; whom shall I fear? The Lord is the strength of my life; of whom shall I be afraid?" *The Lord* means the Presence of God within you. There is no power to challenge God, for God is Almighty. The thing you fear has no power; it is a false belief; it is the bogeyman under the stairs and has no reality. Repeat these wonderful words: "God hath not given us the Spirit of fear; but of power, and of love, and of a sound mind."

7

The second step: You overcome fear by faith in God and all things good. Faith is not a creed, a dogma, or a religion. Faith is a way of thinking; it is a positive mental attitude. Faith is

vital; it is a deep, abiding conviction in God. Faith is the greatest medicine in the world! Take this spiritual medicine of faith now! Look at these words, repeat them: " 'I do all things through Christ which strengtheneth me.' God is with me now. God and His Holy Angels are always with me. I am surrounded by the circle of God's Love." These words are now reflected in your brain and deeper mind. Repeat these powerful statements, and all fear will leave you.

The third step: When fear thoughts come, think of God; imagine you are now resting in the arms of Almighty God in the same way as you rested in your loving mother's arms. Say lovingly to your Father within, "Now, God, I am going about my business, and you are going with me. Your Love, Light, and Power comfort, guide, and bless me in all ways. I love my Father, and my Father loves me; my Father *is* God! It is wonderful!"

OVERCOME WORRY

Worry is due to a lack of faith in God. The person who worries is always expecting things to go wrong. He broods or worries over a great many things that never happen. Such a person tells you all the reasons why something bad should happen, and not one reason why something good should happen. This constant worry debilitates his entire system, resulting in physical and mental disorders.

Your *worry can be cured.* Do not spend time looking at your troubles or problems; cease all negative thinking. Your mind will not work when it is tense. It relieves the strain to do something soothing and pleasant when you are presented with a problem. You do not fight a problem, but you *can* overcome it. ·

To release pressure, take a drive; go for a walk; play solitaire; read a favorite chapter of the Bible, such as the eleventh chapter of Hebrews, or 1 Corinthians 13; or turn to the forty-sixth Psalm; read it over carefully and quietly several times. An inner calm will steal over you, and you are ready to pray.

THREE STEPS IN OVERCOMING WORRY

The first step: Every morning when you awaken turn to God in prayer as you would to your loving Father. Relax the body, then talk to God, the only Presence and the only Power. Become as a little child, this means that you realize God is within you, you trust Him completely. *"God in the midst of you is Mighty to heal."*

The second step: You know in your heart that you can present your problems or difficulties to this Power, and that the Wisdom of God will solve them for you. Say lovingly: "Thank you, Father, for this wonderful day. It is God's day, it is filled with joy, peace, happiness, and success for me. I look forward with a happy expectancy to this day. The Wisdom and Understanding of God will govern me during the entire day. God is my partner, everything I do will turn out in a wonderful way. I believe in God, I trust God."

The third step: You are full of confidence and faith. Now let go, and let God work through you. Remember as you go through your day: "This is the day God made for me! There is Divine activity taking place in my life."

DESIRE—THE GIFT OF GOD

GOD SPEAKS to you through desire. All things begin with desire, it is sometimes called the fountain of all action. As you read this, you have within you the urge or desire to be greater than you are. There is a Cosmic urge within you seeking expression. Life seeks to express its unity, wholeness, love, and beauty through you. You are an instrument of the Divine, you are a channel for Life and Love. You are here to release the imprisoned splendor within you.

Without desire you could not move from your chair. Man desires shelter, and he proceeds to build houses to protect himself from the inclemencies of the season. Man plants seeds of corn and wheat in the ground, because he desires food for his family and himself.

9

You have a supreme desire now; perhaps it is for health, true place, or abundance. Desire unduly prolonged results in frustration and sickness. To desire something good and wonderful over a long period of time, and not attain it, is to waste away in spirit and body. You should learn to realize your desire through prayer; the realization of your desire is your saviour.

THREE STEPS IN REALIZING YOUR DESIRE

The first step: Your desire for harmony, peace, health, true place, wealth, etc., is the voice of God speaking to you. Say from your heart, "With God all things are possible." God is the Living Spirit Almighty within you from which all things flow.

The second step: I am aware _of my desire; I know it exists in the Invisible for me. I claim it is mine now; I accept it in my own mind. I have released my desire into the Creative Medium

within me, which is the source of all things. I claim and believe that my desire is now impressed in my deeper mind. What is impressed must be expressed; this is the way my mind works.

The third step: I now feel the reality of my fulfilled desire. I am at peace. I know in my heart that what I have accepted as true will come to pass. I rejoice and give thanks. My whole being thrills to the reality of the fulfilled desire. I am at peace. God is peace. Thank you, Father; it is done.

HAPPY MARRIAGE

"WHAT GOD HATH joined together, let no man put asunder." A husband and wife should each be married to God and all things good. A husband and wife should never let the sun go down on their wrath. Never carry over from one day to another accumulated irritations arising from little disagreements. Be sure to forgive each other for any sharpness before you retire at night.

The answer to a happy marriage is for each one to see the Christ in the other; begin *now* to see the Presence of the Living God in each other. Say to yourself now, "I salute the Divinity in my husband" or "in my wife," as the case may be. Say to your wife or husband, "I appreciate all you are doing, and I radiate love and goodwill to you all day long." Do not take your marriage partner for granted; show your appreciation and your love.

Think appreciation and goodwill rather than condemnation, criticism, and nagging. Remember the injunction of the Bible, "Except the Lord build the house, they labor in vain that build it." The way to build a peaceful home and a happy marriage is upon the basis of love, beauty, harmony, mutual respect, faith in God, and in all things good.

Say from your heart, "My marriage is consecrated in prayer and love." A husband and wife should always pray together at least once a day, preferably at night before retiring; this will restore peace in the home and in the heart; for God is peace.

THREE STEPS TO A HAPPY MARRIAGE

The first step: In the beginning, God. The moment you awaken in the morning, claim God is guiding you in all ways. Send out loving thoughts of peace, harmony, and love to your marriage partner, to all members of the family, and to the whole world.

The second step: Say grace at breakfast. Give thanks for the wonderful food, for your abundance, and for *all* of your blessings. Make sure that no problem, worries, or arguments shall enter into the table conversation; the same applies at dinner time.

The third step: Husband and wife should alternate in praying each night. Keep the Bible close at hand. Read the 23rd, 91st, 27th Psalms, the 11th Chapter of Hebrews, the 13th Chapter of 1 Corinthians, and other great texts of the New Testament before going to sleep. Say quietly, "Thank you, Father, for all the blessings of the day. God giveth his beloved sleep."

THE SECRET OF PEACE OF MIND

COMMUNION WITH GOD is the way to peace of mind; this means turning to God in prayer and realizing that His Peace and Love are now flowing through your mind and heart. Prayer, or this silent communion with God within you, will change your character. Prayer makes you a different person.

The word *prayer* may be understood as including any form of communion with God whether vocal or mental. Peace of mind is achieved by getting a real sense of the Presence of God within you. In trying to bring peace into the lives of others, your personal opinion is usually wrong. By interfering in their strife, you usually make matters worse. By getting them to patch up their differences or arriving at a compromise to which they agree, there is no true peace, because they have not completely forgiven each other. The best way to heal quarrels of this nature is the silent way of prayer.

Realize that the Wisdom, Love, and Peace of God are flowing through the minds and hearts of all concerned; the trouble will dissolve in a wonderful way. *"Blessed are the peacemakers, for they shall be called the children of God."*

THREE STEPS TO PEACE OF MIND

The first step: Realize God is Peace, and that He dwells in the midst of you; then think of that inner peace as yours now. Say quietly several times: "The Peace of God that passeth all understanding now floods my mind and heart."

The second step: Know that you have in your mind that which you constantly practice. Say frequently during the day, "I know that peace of mind is mine, because I enthrone thoughts of peace, harmony, and goodwill in my mind; I live with these ideas all day long."

The third step: Read the twenty-third Psalm every night; relax the body; say, "I now enthrone in my mind thoughts of peace, love, and goodwill. God is my shepherd, and God's river of peace flows through me now. I lay me down in peace to sleep, for thou, Lord, only maketh me to dwell in safety."

YOU CAN HAVE A BETTER FUTURE

REMEMBER WHAT JAMES said: "Faith without works is dead." You must demonstrate your faith. Faith is a way of thinking, an attitude of mind, a positive, affirmative approach toward life.

If you live, for example, in the joyous expectancy of the best, invariably the best will come to you. You are demonstrating to the world that your faith is in all things good.

Live in the firm conviction of your oneness with God, with Life, and with the Universe. You will find yourself attracting to you wonderful people, greater prosperity, and increased awareness of God's Wisdom. Claim every day of your life that Divine Intelligence is directing your footsteps along the right path; know that God is your source of supply; He is the giver of every perfect gift. Realize that all of your needs are met, and that there is a Divine surplus.

To attain peace and harmony, say from your heart every morning as you arise, "God's peace, the peace that passeth all understanding, fills my mind and heart." Paul says that all things work together for good to them that love God. God and good are synonymous. You are in tune with all things God-like, and behold, *"If any man be in Christ, he is a new creature."*

THREE STEPS TO A BETTER FUTURE

The first step: In all thy ways acknowledge Him, and He will make plain thy path; trust also in Him, and believe in Him, and He will bring it to pass. Turn to God within you; claim that God is governing all of your affairs.

The second step: Realize that the way to get along with people and adjust yourself to life is to love them. Let your heart

be motivated by love and goodwill toward all around you. Pray for the peace and prosperity of all of those with whom you are associated.

The third step: Have a definite mental attitude of success. When presented with a problem, realize that the Infinite Intelligence of God is revealing to you the perfect plan and showing you the way you should go. As you go to sleep say, "God knows the answer." *Feel* the joy of the answered prayer.

OVERCOME IRRITATION

"He whose spirit is without restraint, is like a city that is broken down and without walls." "He that ruleth his spirit is greater than he that taketh a city."

In order that you might lead a full and happy life, control of the emotions is essential. To govern and control your emotions and temper tantrums, it is essential to maintain control over your thoughts. As a matter of fact, you cannot find peace any other way. Willpower or mental coercion will not do it. Forcing yourself to suppress your anger is not the way.

The answer is to enthrone God-like thoughts in your mind, busy yourself mentally with the concepts of peace, harmony, and goodwill. Keep firm control over your thoughts. Learn to substitute love for fear, and peace for discord.

You can direct your thoughts along harmonious lines. For example, if you see or hear of something that disturbs or angers you, instead of giving way to anger or irritation, say automatically, "The peace of God that passeth all understanding is now flooding my mind, my body, and my whole being." Repeat this phrase several times during the period of stress, you will find that all tension and anger disappear.

Fill your mind with Love, and the negative thoughts cannot enter. When someone says something sharp or critical to you, think on a single statement of Truth, such as, "God is Love. He leadeth me beside the still waters." Peace steals over you, you will radiate this peace.

THREE STEPS IN OVERCOMING IRRITATION

The first step: As you awaken in the morning, say to yourself: "This is God's day; it is a new day for me, a new beginning. The restoring, healing, soothing, loving power of God is flowing through me, bringing peace to my mind and body now and forevermore."

The second step: Should some business problem or some person upset or irritate you, think immediately about His Holy Presence. Say, "God is with me all day. His peace, His Guidance, and His Love enable me to meet all problems calmly and peacefully."

The third step: Radiate Love to all of your associates. Claim that they are doing their best. Say, "I wish them peace, harmony, and joy. I salute the God in them." And lo and behold, God and His Love come forth!

YOUR SPIRITUAL REBIRTH

WHEN THE STORM of life disturbs you, and it appears that your ship is about to founder, remember that it is time for you to awaken to the Christ within. This is how you become reborn spiritually: Recall to mind that God is within you, the very

life of you. "Closer is He than breathing, nearer is He than hands and feet." Realize that "With God all things are possible." Claim and know that the God-Power within you is able to cope with any difficulty. Dwell on the peace and harmony of God where the difficulty is, and a perfect, Divine solution will follow.

If troubled, say, "Peace, be still!" The peace of God will steal over you. Turn your burdens (your problems) over to the God-Wisdom within you, knowing and believing that the perfect solution will come to you in God's own way. When you do this with faith and confidence, the storm or anxiety will pass away, and a great calm will steal over you; this is the peace that passeth all understanding. If you are living in limitation and sickness, this is bondage and restriction; it means you are in the dark as to the higher side of life

16

and your tremendous potentialities. When you catch a glimpse of a higher set of facts, the old way of thinking will be displaced; then your Christ or inner Life will rise from the dead, or limited state.

Enthrone the concepts of peace, harmony, and success in your mind; busy your mind with these things; you will find that your body and circumstances will reflect your inner, mental attitude; this is the new birth of freedom. Remove prejudices, deceit, and jealousies from your mind by opening your mind to the Light of God's Love and inspiration. God's Love revivifies and thrills you; this is the birth of God in you.

THREE STEPS TO YOUR SPIRITUAL REBIRTH

The first step: "I saw a new heaven and a new earth." I know now that God's Love springs in my soul. My heart feels the Presence of God, because I radiate Love and joy to all.

The second step: Any time a negative, fearful, critical thought comes to me, I say, "God is with me." This kills it; then my soul is filled with Love toward all.

The third step: Remember always that God never changes. God is within you—your loving Father—saying, "Fear not, child, for all is thine!"

Love Is Freedom

The Pharisees also came unto him, tempting him, and saying unto him, Is it lawful for a man to put away his wife for every cause? And he answered and said unto them, Have ye not read, that he which made them at the beginning made them male and female, and said, For this cause shall a man leave father and mother, and shall cleave to his wife: and they twain shall be one flesh? Wherefore they are no more twain, but one flesh. What therefore God hath joined together, let no man put asunder. . . . Whoever shall put away his wife, except it be for fornication, and shall marry another, committeth adultery: and whoso marrieth her which is put away doth commit adultery.
—Matthew 19:3-6, 9

LET US SEE these great truths in a new light. God is love, and when true love in the heart unites a man and a woman together, that is actually God joining a couple in a sacred covenant. When there is a true, spiritual union between two people *(God hath joined)*, there is-no divorce, for none is wanted. They blend spiritually, mentally, and physically.

There is no institution on earth so sacred as that of the home you are about to make and no vows so wonderful as those you make in the marriage ceremony. True marriage is the holiest of all earthly institutions. It should be entered into reverently, thoughtfully, and with a deep understanding of its spiritual significance. Marriage is an accord of Divine ideas, a harmony and purity of purpose. Harmony, honesty, love, and integrity must prevail in the minds and hearts of both husband and wife. From this inner state of conscious unity in these essential characteristics of a successful marriage there comes the outer state which corresponds to it, making the outer like the inner—peaceful, joyous, and harmonious.

When a man marries a woman because of her wealth, social standing, and political connections, or merely because she is young and beautiful and he wishes to exalt his ego, this is not a real marriage. Actually, it is a sham and a farce. When a woman marries a man because of his profession or for her own personal security or for any reason other than real love, such a marriage is

18

false and a masquerade; it is not made in heaven, meaning harmony and Divine understanding.

I have performed marriage ceremonies for men and women of advanced years, sometimes blessed with as many as seventy-five to eighty years, chronologically speaking. The fires of sex have died out in many of these cases; nevertheless, God (love) joins them together for the simple reason that they are honest, just, sincere, and truthful with each other, and they seek a loving companionship where they desire to share their joys and experiences together. Honesty, sincerity, integrity, and justice are children of love, and when these are absent in the marriage ceremony, regardless of age, it is not a true marriage.

A minister, rabbi, or priest officiating at the ceremony does not validate or sanctify a marriage. He merely confirms objectively what the man and woman already felt to be true subjectively, which was a union of two souls seeking their way back to the heart of God.

How often is marriage a real spiritual union where the parties to the contract blend themselves spiritually, mentally, and physically? And, on the other hand, how often is it a legal ceremony against which the husband and wife begin to chafe in a few weeks? Remember that like attracts like, and if you want to attract the right companion, use the proven spiritual approach as follows: Still your mind, think clearly and with interest on the qualities and attributes you admire in a man or woman, and mentally dwell on the characteristics that you would admire in the other, such as whether he or she is spiritual, loyal, faithful, honest, talented, happy, and prosperous. Gradually these qualities will sink into your subconscious mind. Infinite intelligence always takes over when you pray this way, and, as a result, you will irresistibly attract to you the right companion. The man or woman whom you attract will be the image and likeness of the ideal on which you meditated. You will harmonize perfectly, and there will be mutual love, freedom, and respect; this is called the "marriage made in heaven," or "peace and understanding."

The question frequently arises, "Should I get a divorce?" This is an individual problem. It cannot be generalized. In some cases, divorce is not the solution any more than marriage is the solution for a lonely man. Divorce may be right for one person and wrong for another. A divorced woman may be far more noble and God-like than many of her sisters who are living a lie rather than facing the truth. The usual excuses and alibis used to cover up are that it would be bad for John's business, or the neighbors would talk, or it would be bad politics, etc. This, of course, is making a mockery of marriage.

Some time ago I talked with a woman who had been deceived and tricked by her husband. He had told her prior to marriage that he was a representative for an eastern concern, that he was single, and that he belonged to her church organization—all lies. It turned out that he was an ex-convict, a wife-beater, and that he was living with another woman when he married her. She had advanced him some money, thereby whetting his taste for more, which is the real reason why he married her. She thought it was a sin, however, to get a divorce, yet she longed for freedom and peace of mind. I explained to her that she was not really married at all, that such a marriage was simply a sham and a mockery, and that she was living a lie. She thereupon proceeded immediately to get a divorce and dissolved this fraudulent marriage forthwith.

I recall the case, during the war, of a young girl who got highly intoxicated one evening, which resulted in a complete blackout, and she found herself with a marriage certificate the next morning. She had married a native of one of the islands. She was shocked beyond words and had to get psychiatric treatment. She immediately dissolved the marriage.

A great number of people are confused and suffer from a guilt complex based on misinterpretation of the biblical quotation, Whosoever shall put away his wife, except it be for fornication, and shall marry another, committeth adultery: and whoso marrieth her which is put away doth commit adultery (Matthew 19:9). The Bible also says: Whosoever looketh on a woman to lust after her hath committed adultery with her already in his heart (Matthew 5:28).

Here we are told that adultery is of the heart or the mind. The heart is the seat of the emotions, the feeling nature, the subjective mind. Acts of the body are determined by the movement of the mind. A hundred years ago, Phineas Parkhurst Quimby pointed out that the body moves as it is moved upon by our mind, and the body acts as it is acted upon.

Fornication in Bible language means giving allegiance and attention to false gods rather than to the one true God—the Living Spirit Almighty within man, which is the supreme and sovereign Power. The Bible is a psychological document; it points out that when man visits the slums in his own mind and keeps company with mental murderers, such as hate, resentment, anger, or ill-will, he is cohabiting with evil and is therefore guilty of fornication and adultery. In biblical language, he is already divorced for the simple reason that he has separated himself from God for his immediate pleasure. He is cohabiting with evil in his mind, and he is no longer married to peace, harmony, love, and understanding.

Man is fornicating when he mentally and emotionally unites with erroneous concepts, indulges in resentment and anger, or becomes morose and morbid. Whenever men and women are mentally divorced from their marriage vows, eventually there will be a separation or divorce on the external plane. The subjective side of life always controls the objective phase of life.

We must remember that just because a man and a woman have a marriage certificate and live in a home, it does not follow necessarily that it is a real home. Perhaps it is a place of discord and hate. When, for example, a child is present and the parents do not know the laws of life, it is better to break up such a union than to have the mood of hate impair the growing mind of the child. Many times a child's life and mind are dwarfed by the mood of the parents, which in the passage of years often results in neurosis and crime. It is far better for a boy to live with one parent who loves him than to live with two who hate each other and who fight all the time.

Many men and women have told me that they feel very guilty because of what they term "sex sins." They feel that God hasn't forgiven them. I explain to them that God is the Life Principle, that Life does not condemn or punish, and that they are simply condemning themselves and suffering accordingly and needlessly.

God is the Life Principle. If you burn your finger, you know very well that the Life Principle forgives you by reducing the edema and by giving you new tissue. Life has no grudge against you for having burned yourself; It forms a blood clot, builds a bridge of new cells, and forms new skin. If you have eaten some bad food, Life forgives you by causing you to regurgitate, thereby cleansing your system of possible food poisoning. Life always seeks to preserve you. This is the meaning of "God does not condemn or punish you." We punish ourselves by the misuse of our subconscious mind.

Jesus said to the woman caught in adultery: Woman, where are those thine accusers? Hath no man condemned thee? She said, No man, Lord. And Jesus said unto her, Neither do I condemn thee: go, and sin no more (John 8:10-11).

The harlot, or the woman with the illegitimate child, who may be condemned and stoned (ostracized) by the world, may turn to the God Presence within and claim her freedom and peace of mind. She realizes that God condemns no one. *Thou art of purer eyes than to behold evil, and canst not look on iniquity* (Habakkuk 1:13). Society and the world may condemn her, or she may engage in self-accusation and self-criticism. *For the Father judgeth no man, but hath committed all judgment unto the Son* (John 5:22).

The *Son* is your mind. This is the place wherein you pronounce judgment on yourself by the thoughts you entertain. God, the Absolute, knows nothing about our errors and fears. You forgive yourself by giving yourself the mood of peace, love, and harmony for the mood of guilt, despair, and self-condemnation.

Turn from the past and completely detach yourself from the former way of living. Mentally and emotionally unite with your aim, which is peace, dignity, happiness, and freedom. As you do, God and His glory responds at once. You will find a wave of peace moving over the arid areas of your mind like the dew of heaven, and the shadows of fear and guilt will pass away. As you cease to condemn yourself, you will find that neither can the world condemn you.

There is nothing evil in sex or in anything else created and ordained by God. *Male and female created he them* (Genesis 1:27). *Therefore shall a man leave his father and his mother, and shall cleave unto his wife: and they shall be one flesh* (Genesis 2:24). In marriage you give yourself completely—spiritually, mentally, and physically. The sex act between husband and wife should be a love act, and each should realize that love is of God and that any children born will be born of that love. The sex instinct is not opposed to spiritual impulses. The sex drive must be channeled constructively, harmoniously, and lovingly. Lust as such is not love; the normal sexual act between marriage partners, however, involves the genuine emotion of love, which is the essence of conjugal love.

Many married men and women have a false, negative attitude toward sex. Some think that it is evil, nasty, and ugly, possibly due to their upbringing or due to some sexual shock in childhood. Often, this attitude results in impotence in men and frigidity in women.

I have had women say to me that their husbands were materialistic and carnal, and that they looked down on their husbands, claiming that they were superior because they despised and hated the sex act. This is pure rationalization and indicates subconscious poison pockets regarding sex, in all probability due to early training and false interpretation of the Scriptures.

A distant relative of mine once told me that before the sex act, she and her husband prayed. There is nothing wrong with prayer, but the reason for their prayer at that time was due to the fact that she looked upon the sexual act as sinful and unclean, and she thought she would exorcise through prayer any evil connected with the act. Basically, she had contempt for sex and was frigid. She said, "I love my husband spiritually, not physically." She separated sexual love from spiritual love.

I explained to her that marriage is a total union of body and soul. *A man . . . shall cleave unto his wife: and they shall be one flesh* (Genesis 2:24).

She thereafter began to affirm, "I love my husband spiritually, mentally, emotionally, and physically. He is God's man, and I radiate love, peace, and goodwill to him. God's love flows from me to him, and our sex relationship is joyous, loving, and harmonious. Between us are mutual love, freedom, and respect."

After a few weeks, her frigidity was dissolved, and there was a harmonious marriage. She intuitively perceived a great truth: God had placed in her heart a desire to attract a man, and He had placed in the man a desire to attract a woman.

A few days ago, I talked to a woman who was about to get her eighth divorce. She was exceedingly bitter and resentful toward her present husband as well as toward all the previous ones. She had remarried each time without forgiving and mentally releasing her husbands, and each one was worse than the preceding one. Her inner mood of resentment had caused her to attract similar types of men, based on the law of attraction. The cure was to forgive herself and all her former husbands and to build into her mentality the mental equivalent of the kind of man she desired.

If you strike a key on a grand piano, all the tones in harmony with it will respond. They may be higher or lower, but they are similar. So too do you attract to yourself those people who have qualities based on your mood and concept of yourself. It is affinity or attraction, depending upon the chord you strike. You may strike a discord, but you do not take out all the discords in order to make a harmony. When you discipline your mind in prayer and enter into the spirit of forgiveness, you can play a divine melody.

Suppose that a man cheats on his wife. If he had love and respect for his wife, he would not want any other woman. When a man has found his true, spiritual ideal in marriage, he has no desire for any other woman. Love is a oneness; it is not a duality or a multiplicity. A man who runs around with many women—which indicates the many adulterous moods within him—is marrying many concepts, such as frustration, resentment, cynicism, etc. When you have found love with your mate, you also have found a fullness of life.

You may ask, "Why did some men previously have many wives?" The reason was that at one time the earth was underpopulated, and the earthly fathers, not knowing anything better, followed this polygamous method. Today, we are more spiritually awakened, and we know that the earth is populated enough.

The philanderer has a profound inferiority complex and feels insecure, and all the women he meets are vacillating, neurotic, and confused like himself. He is seeing and hearing his own inner vibrations. "Birds of a feather flock together." "Like begets like."

Let us take the case of the woman who is running around with a married man. Such a woman has been unable to demonstrate a husband or a boyfriend, she gets a pseudo-satisfaction, or false thrill, in stealing another woman's husband. She, too, has an inferiority complex and is unstable.

Man demotes himself by his feeling of lack and limitation. His fear is transmitted to his wife, and she reacts in kind. She cannot see him in the way she formerly did, as he has not the same feeling about himself. She can see him only in the way he sees himself; likewise, he can see her only in the way she sees herself.

If a man feels himself to be dignified, he commands respect and he gets it. A man who has the predominant mood of success and happiness knits together all the members of his household. He is a cementing influence, and there is harmony and peace in his household.

The sex life prevails in the vegetable, animal, and human life. Basically, it is the life force seeking expression in all its varied forms. The sex urge is operating in you through your talents, abilities, feelings, and urges. Whenever you meditate on the truths of God, or upon any idea, and enter into the feeling of it, that also is a phase of sex. Your hunger and thirst for truth, your spiritual awareness and understanding, and your intense desire to reproduce more and more of the goodness of God in the land of the living—these are all spiritual outlets for the sex urge or life force within you.

When you are not fully expressed along all lines and when you do not constructively channel your libido or life force, the emotions become dammed up and bottled up, resulting in frustration, neurosis, imbalance, mental disorders, and in forms of escape in alcoholism and drug addiction.

A man once boasted to me that he had not had relations with his wife for over four years, and he added that he had become more *spiritual.* He belonged to a strange cult, the leader of which had told him that in order to advance spiritually, he had to lead an ascetic life and refrain from all intercourse with his wife. This man was neurotic, afflicted with ulcers, and mentally disturbed. He had been brainwashed into believing that sex was evil and would inhibit his spiritual illumination. I explained to him that all this was pure balderdash and primitive thinking based on ignorance, superstition, and fear of sex.

At my suggestion he renewed normal relations with his wife, looking upon the act as right. He realized that he was God-placed in this world to enjoy all of his senses and to go forth and multiply and replenish the earth. Wise use of our faculties, urges, and desires in moderation in all things is the answer—not repression or suppression. Thereafter his constant prayer was: "We have a happy, joyous marriage, satisfying and harmonious, of true and lasting love. Divine love reigns supreme in our marriage now." Their marriage has been much happier than ever before.

If love is lacking in your life, use this prayer frequently: "God's love, wisdom, and harmony are being expressed through me now. Poise, balance, and equilibrium reign supreme in my life." As you make a habit of this prayer, wonders will happen in your life. Love, inspiration, and guidance will well up spontaneously, and you will become an irresistible magnet attracting to you all the blessings of life from all directions.

Young men and women often ask me if they should experiment before marriage. I tell them that marriage does not change anything and that if they freely indulge before marriage, how can they expect fidelity or trust after marriage?

A young man who was studying physics in New York went in for free love. "Morals," he said, "are a joke." He had no standards, and he was having sexual relations with several girls who attended the same college. One girl became pregnant. Then there followed legal action and a "shotgun" wedding. He had to quit college in order to take care of his wife: he worked as a waiter. He had married a girl he didn't want, and a baby was born that neither of them wanted. Where are his freedom and his free love? He has placed himself in the prison of want, lack, resentment, and poverty.

You are aware that you must curb your appetite for alcohol, fats, ice cream, and cigarettes. Likewise, you must curb your emotions, urges, and drives, and you must see that they are expressed harmoniously and wisely. Your sex life must be blended with love and understanding.

Premarital sexual experiences are not conducive to a happy married life. Often, the man distrusts the woman he can have so easily. He says to himself, "If she will do this before marriage, she will do it with others afterwards." I ask a young man, "Is your girlfriend nobler, grander, sweeter, more dignified in your eyes now than before sex relations?" Usually, he blushes and says, "No, I guess you're right."

Happiness in marriage depends on love, loyalty, honesty, devotion to the truth, integrity, and a desire to lift up each other spiritually, mentally, and in all ways. Love does not take a woman to a shabby motel, neither is real love experienced furtively by an illicit interlude in such a cheap motel.

To maintain a happy married life, pray together and you will stay together. Affirm frequently: "Divine love, harmony, peace, and perfect understanding are now operating and expressed in our heavenly marriage. Morning, noon, and night we salute the Divinity in each other, and all our ways are ways of pleasantness and all our paths are peace."

27

Mental Poisons and Their Antidotes

RIGHT MENTAL ATTITUDE INDUCES HEALING

THERE ARE MENTAL as well as physical poisons. Mental poisons are wrong thoughts which work underground in consciousness like a contaminated stream to emerge even after years in wrong experiences (illness, loss, unhappiness, etc.).

I read some time ago of a scientific experiment in Russia in which six hypnotized and conditioned cats were given cyanide of potassium with no fatal effects, while six other unconditioned animals all died. If we had enough faith in the subjective power of God within ourselves, we could nullify all deadly poisons, mental and otherwise.

What is the prophylaxis? The first step is not to be afraid of the cancer, tuberculosis, arthritis, or mental disorder from this moment. The second step is to realize that the condition is the product of false thinking and will have no more power to continue its existence; then you are exalting the God in the midst of you. This will stop all toxicity in you or the person for whom you are praying.

Pronounce the condition "false" and exalt God by seeing the perfect solution, the beauty, and wholeness made manifest where the trouble is.

Among the most deadly mental poisons are the following: Fear, hatred, self pity, resentment, envy, vengeance, loneliness, and melancholy. All these are modifications of fear. The biblical name for fear is a blind, false thought called Goliath. The word *Goliath* means an aggressive, domineering thought or idea that brags about its power, intimidates, bullies, browbeats, and frightens you into submission to its unrighteous reign. Perhaps you are afraid to meet this gangster, intruder, or marauder in your mind. Maybe you are afraid of results, and you hesitate to meet this sinister shadow openly and rout him out.

It is necessary to play the role of David in order to get rid of this ganster called fear. *David* means a man who loves God, who knows there is only One Sovereign Power which moves as a Unity and knows no divisions or quarrels, and whose name is Love. David, which is your awareness of the Presence and Power of God, killed the Philistine giant called Goliath, or fear, with a stone thrown from his shepherd's sling. Fear is a shadow of the mind held by ignorance and darkness. When you hold your fear to the light of reason and intelligence, it can't stand the light and it disappears. Among the offspring of fear are the following:

Hatred, which is really inverted or misdirected love based on ignorance.

Self-pity, which is really self-absorption. This mental poison creeps through the psychic bloodstream poisoning the springs of hope and faith, leading to dementia praecox, melancholia, etc. The antidote is to find your *other* self (God) and become intoxicated by realizing your love of God, and your sense of union with the One Power will bring about a new birth of peace, health, confidence, and strength.

Old-age fear is another mental poison. Old age is not the flight of years, but the dawn of wisdom, truth, and beauty.

Loneliness is a lack of love. The loveless seek love, but the loving find love and friendship everywhere. The antidote is to fall in love with God's companions in your mind. Their names are goodwill, kindness, gentleness, peace, patience, understanding, and a sincere interest in others. Pour out God's Love—a double portion of the Spirit—on those around you; then you will banish loneliness immediately. God will give you a double reward also, and your good will be multiplied exceedingly.

29

Your state of mind is your master. It is foolish to let that ignorant, blind, stupid monster fear push you around and direct your activities. Consider yourself too smart, too brilliant, for that to happen. Why not become David? Play the role; it will pay you fabulous dividends. David means your faith in God is greater than fear. Fear is faith upside down. Fear is a conglomeration of dark and sinister shadows in the mind. In short, fear is faith in the wrong thing. Become a spiritual giant, call David forth (which is confidence in God). He is within you; summon him. At the same time you can call forth God's Love.

The children of faith in God are love, peace, gentleness, goodness, kindness, joy, balance, tranquillity, and serenity.

When you realize that there is but One Power, One Cause—the Maker—you give all your allegiance, devotion, and loyalty to

that One; then you become David, beloved of God. David (spiritual awareness) had no armor or material protection such as they used in those days. His power was his trust in the God of his fathers, knowing that Infinite Intelligence knew only the answer to any problem.

When you claim God's guidance and God's direction, you will always see the weak spots in the armor of Goliath or the person who threatens you with dire disaster. Actually it is never the person who has the power, but the thought in your own mind. The enemies are of thine own household (mind). *And David put his hand in his bag, and took thence a stone, and slang it, and smote the Philistine in his forehead, that the stone sunk into his forehead; and he fell upon his face to the earth* (1 Samuel 17:49). The stone is your conviction of the One God, the One Power. A stone is hard and impervious, which means that your faith or confidence in the Spiritual Power is unyielding and inflexible. In other words you are unmoved, undisturbed, unyielding in your attitude, and you trust in the One, the Beautiful, and the Good. With this stone or mental conviction you shatter the forehead of the giant called fear or Goliath. Fear is prone to brag, and in that lies its weakness. David (love of Truth) went forth with one idea: to prove the supremacy of the God-Power. When you go forth in the assurance that "one with God is a

30

majority," you will find yourself guided in every way and you will become the inevitable victor.

Don't fight fear with fear, instead meet it with a direct declaration of God's Presence and Power, which renders fear powerless. Say to yourself, "The Lord is my light and my salvation; whom shall I fear? The Lord is the strength of my life; of whom shall I be afraid?" (Psalm 27:1, 2). Are you afraid of some disease which has gripped you? You will notice that an erroneous thought in your mind can brag and boast of its pseudo-strength and it intimidates you. Don't let these thoughts bully and browbeat you. Meet and subdue them now. Realize that all discord is manufactured by your own mind; it is not something you catch on the outside. You can change your mind by realizing that the Infinite Healing Presence which made your body is healing it now. As you do this consciously and knowingly, there will be a rearrangement of the thought-patterns in your subconscious, and a healing will follow. Your present mental conviction determines your future and your experience.

Meditate and pray upon positive and spiritual values. Claim your ideal, solution, health, or peace of mind upon the basis that the Spirit within you is Supreme and Omnipotent, and by thinking of your solution or ideal with confidence and faith, you are conditioning your mind to the answer. Your mind is full of confidence or fear according to what you put into it. Become David, the ruddy-faced shepherd boy, by partaking of and appropriating your Divinity now. Get the insight to persevere and know that you will meet on life's journey only those experiences which you consciously and unconsciously send before you. Claim that God and His Love go before you; this means the mood of confidence, faith, and trust in an Almighty Power which never faileth. As you do this, you are David going forth in might and right, clothed with the whole armor of God, preparing for yourself freedom, peace of mind, and happiness.

The story in Samuel tells us that David cut the head off Goliath. This is what the spiritually minded man must do with all error, false belief, and superstitions in his mind; he must cremate, burn up, and consume all negative thoughts with the fire of Divine Love and right thinking. Goliath or fear is faith in a false god. You are David properly equipped when you realize you have faith in the One True God—the only Power and Presence.

Recently I was talking to a husband and wife who were convinced that they would lose everything in a lawsuit which had dragged on for five years. They were very pessimistic; it seemed the other side were lying and were, as the saying goes, trying to get something for nothing. Their lawyer told them that in his opinion they didn't stand a chance, and they were hypnotized by that suggestion. I explained to them that the statement or suggestion of the lawyer had no power and that his words could not bring to pass what he suggested. They realized that the only power the suggestion of their attorney had was their mental acceptance of it. They had accepted the suggestion and had reacted accordingly, but the whole process took place in their own poisons and neutralizing the toxic effects with right thinking and right feeling. She placed God back on the throne of her mind, saying to herself, "I will fear no evil: for thou art with me" (Psalm 23:41.

Where God is there can be no evil, and as she saturated her mind with the simple truth, "God is; His Presence fills my soul and rules my life," all the ill-will vanished away. She positively refused to let some other woman give her migraine, indigestion, insomnia, and the jitters. No one has that power. The power is in your own thought-life. You are the one to determine how your thought moves. Good and evil are the movements of our own mind. Do not permit thieves of fear, resentment, and inadequacy to restrict, bind, and hold you in the chains of bondage. The world we see is really the world we are. We see through the mental pictures and convictions of our subconscious mind. We color everything by our inner conditioning. Man projects his feelings, prejudices, and animosities onto people and he forms a twisted, distorted picture of everything.

Define your goal now. Where are you going? What is your objective? Get a definite plan or purpose; then claim God is moving in your behalf. Whenever any negative suggestion quarrels with you relative to the goal in your mind, chop its head off incisively and decisively with your spiritual sword of reason, which tells you that there is but One Spiritual Power and that the God who gave you the desire is the same God who fulfills it. It is easy, for the "Father indwelling, He doeth the works." No one has the power to upset you or take away your faith and confidence in He Who Is. Raise your sights! Let your vision be on the goal, the summit you wish to reach, and you will go to the place where your vision is.

Become David by falling in love with God's Truths and trust completely the Infinite Wisdom to show you the solution. Know that God in action in you brings you beauty, peace, Divine right place, and harmony. David was the son of Jesse, which means minds. They permitted their attorney to suggest the loss of the case to them. All the time the power was in their own thought. They prayed as follows: "God is Absolute Harmony and Absolute Justice; therefore the result is justice, harmony, and satisfaction to everybody." This was their simple prayer. Their premise was true; therefore the conclusion had to be true. Moreover, the beginning and the end were the same. If a man begins with God he ends with God, or the Good. The fruit is in the seed, the oak is in the acorn. There was a perfect, harmonious solution to the lawsuit and it was settled out of court.

God is never late; the secret is in remaining loyal and faithful to that which you know to be true of God. Do not hesitate to draw the sword of Truth like David. Become armed with spiritual reasoning and understanding of Divine Law and the Eternal Verities. Slay ruthlessly and without pity all negative thought-patterns in your mind; order them out in a dynamic, forceful way, and let in the Light, Love, and Truth of God. Your spiritual awareness acts as a sword in that it severs you completely from the old way of thinking, race belief, other powers, malefic entities, and suppositional opposites to the One Supreme, Loving Power.

A woman said to me last week, "I am so mad, I could kill May!" It seems May had spread lies about her and had also tried to undermine her in the position she held. The woman permitted May to disturb her; in other words, she gave power to May which May did not possess. The trouble was in her own thought-life. May was not responsible for the way she was thinking about her; she

33

realized suddenly that the whole trouble was in her own mental imagery and thought-patterns. She let Goliath (fear) run riot in her own mind, browbeating, intimidating, bullying, and frightening her—the whole process being one of her own creation. The_young lady had good common sense and she began to vent her spleen on the bacteria of fear, hatred, and resentment in her mind, casting out these mental poisons and neutralizing the toxic effects with right thinking and right feeling. She placed God back on the throne of her mind, saying to herself, "I will fear no evil: for thou art with me" (Psalm 23:4).

Where God is there can be no evil, and as she saturated her mind with the simple truth, "God is, His Presence fills my soul and rules my life," all the ill-will vanished away. She positively refused to let some other woman give her migraine, indigestion, insomnia, and the jitters. No one has that power. The power is in your own thought-life. You are the one to determine how your thought moves. Good and evil are the movements of our own mind. Do not permit thieves of fear, resentment, and inadequacy to restrict, bind, and hold you in the chains of bondage. The world we see is really the world we are. We see through the mental pictures and convictions of our subconscious mind. We color everything by our inner conditioning. Man projects his feelings, prejudices, and animosities onto people and he forms a twisted, distorted picture of everything.

Define your goal now. Where are you going? What is your objective? Get a definite plan or purpose, then claim God is moving in your behalf. Whenever any negative suggestion quarrels with you relative to the goal in your mind, chop its head off incisively and decisively with your spiritual sword of reason, which tells you that there is but One Spiritual Power and that the God who gave you the desire is the same God who fulfills it. It is easy, for the "Father indwelling, He doeth the works." No one has the power to upset you or take away your faith and confidence in He Who Is. Raise your sights! Let your vision be on the goal, the summit you wish to reach, and you will go to the place where your vision is.

Become David by falling in love with God's Truths and trust completely the Infinite Wisdom to show you the solution. Know that God in action in you brings you beauty, peace, Divine right place, and harmony. David was the son of Jesse, which means the son of I Am or God. So are YOU the son of the Infinite and the child of Eternity. Draw close to your Father. He loves you and He cares for you! As you turn to Him, He will turn to you, then the dawn appears and all the shadows flee away.

The Wonders of Inner Speech

Let the words of my mouth, and the meditation of my heart, be acceptable in thy sight, O Lord, my strength, and my redeemer.
—Psalm 19:14

WONDERS WILL HAPPEN in your life when your inner thought and feeling agree with the words of your mouth. Apropos of this I should like to cite the following case: A man was involved in a long-delayed lawsuit which had cost him considerable time, legal fees, etc. He was exasperated, bitter, and hostile toward the opposition and his own attorneys. His inner speech, which represents his inner, silent, unexpressed thoughts, was more or less as follows: "It's hopeless! This has gone on for five years. I am being sold down the river. It is useless to go on. I might as well give up," etc. I explained to him that this inner speech was highly destructive and was undoubtedly playing a major role in prolonging the case. Job said, *For the thing which I greatly feared is come upon me* (Job 3:25).

He changed his inner and outer speech completely when he fully understood what he had been doing to himself. Actually he had been praying against himself. I asked him a single question as follows: "What would you say if I told you this minute that there had been a perfect, harmonious solution reached and the whole matter was concluded?"

He replied, "I would be delighted and eternally grateful. I would feel wonderful knowing that the whole thing was finished."

He agreed from that moment on to see to it that his inner speech, as Ouspensky pointed out, would agree with his aim. Regularly and systematically he applied the following prayer which I gave him: "I give thanks for the perfect, harmonious solution which came through the wisdom of the All-Wise One." He repeated this to himself frequently during the day, and when difficulties, delays, setbacks, arguments, doubt, and fear came to his mind, he would silently affirm the above truth. He ceased completely making all negative statements verbally and also watched his inner speech, knowing that his inner speech would always be made manifest. It is what we feel on the inside that is expressed. We can say one thing with the mouth and feel another in our heart, it is what we feel that is reproduced on the screen of space. We must never affirm inwardly what we do not want to experience outwardly. The lips and the heart should agree; when they do, our prayer is answered.

We must watch our inner psychological state. Some people mutter to themselves, are envious, jealous, seething with anger and hostility. Such a mental attitude is highly destructive and brings chaos, sickness, and lack in its train. You are familiar with the person who justifies himself; he tells himself that he has a perfect right to be angry, seek revenge, and try to get even. He is playing an old subconscious phonograph record which recites all the alibis, excuses, and justification for his inner boiling state. In all probability he does not know that such a mental state causes him to lose psychic energy on a large scale, rendering him inefficient and confused. Man's negative inner speech is usually directed against some person.

I talked to a man recently who told me that he had been treated shabbily; how he planned to get even; how hateful he was toward his former employer, etc. This man had ulcers of the stomach as a result of his inner turmoil and irritation. I explained to him that he had been making very destructive impressions of anger and resentment on his subconscious mind, which always expresses what is impressed upon it. These destructive emotions must have an outlet, and they came forth as ulcers and neurosis in his case.

He reversed his mental processes by releasing his former employer into the boundless ocean of God's Love and wishing for him all the blessings of Heaven. At the same time he filled his mind with the Truths of God by identifying himself with the Infinite Healing Presence, realizing that the Harmony, Peace, and Perfection of the Infinite One were saturating his mind and body, making him every whit whole. These spiritual vibrations permeating his mind were transmitted throughout his entire system, and the cells of his body took on a new spiritual tone resulting in a healing of his discordant condition.

The Bible says, *If two of you shall agree on earth as touching anything that they shall ask, it shall be done for them of my Father which is in heaven.* Who are these two? It means you and your desire; i.e., if you accept your desire mentally, the subconscious mind will bring it to pass, because your conscious and subconscious have agreed or synchronized. The two agreeing represent your thought and feeling, your idea and emotion. If you succeed in emotionalizing the concept, the male and female aspect of your mind have agreed and there will be an issue or mental offspring, namely the answered prayer.

It must be recalled that whatever we accept or feel as true is impregnated in our subconscious mind. The subconscious is the creative medium; its tendency, as Troward points out, is always lifeward. The subconscious controls all your vital organs, is the seat of memory, and the healer of the body. The subconscious is fed by hidden springs and is one with Infinite Intelligence and Infinite Power.

It is very important to give the proper instruction to the subconscious. For example, if a man dwells on obstacles, delays, difficulties, and obstructions to his program, the subconscious will take that as his request and proceed to bring difficulties and disappointments into his experience; hence, feed the subconscious with premises which are true.

What kind of inner talking goes on in you all the time which is not being expressed audibly? It is your inner talking that the subconscious listens to and obeys. Your subconscious records your silent thought and feeling, and it is a very faithful recording machine. It records everything and plays the record back to you in the form of experiences, conditions, and events. You do not have to travel psychologically with fear, doubt, anxiety, and anger. There is no law which says that you have to travel with gangsters, assassins, murderers, intruders, and thieves in your mind. If you continue to invite such thieves and robbers into your mind, they rob you of your health, happiness, peace and prosperity, and make you a physical and mental wreck.

A woman had a blood pressure of over two hundred accompanied by severe migraine attacks; the cause of all this was destructive inner speech. She felt that someone had not treated her right and she became very negative toward that other person. She justified herself in being hostile and antagonistic toward this other person, allowing this condition to go on for weeks, and she was in a deep emotional stew. This negative attitude drained force from her, bringing about psychological changes in her bloodstream. She was ready, as she said, to explode with anger. This inner pressure, mounting tension, and seething hostility were the cause of her high blood pressure or hypertension plus the migraine.

This woman began to practice the wonders of spiritual inner speech. She realized she had been poisoning herself and that the other woman was in no way responsible for the way she was thinking or feeling about her. She was the only thinker in her universe, and she had been thinking vicious, destructive, malicious thoughts which were poisoning her whole system. She began to comprehend and see that no one could possibly touch her except through her own thought- or the movement of her own mind. All she had to do in order to practice the wonders of true spiritual inner speech was to identify with her aim. Her aim was peace, health, happiness, joy, serenity, and tranquillity. She began to identify with God's River of Peace and God's Love flowing through her like a golden yellow river soothing, healing, and restoring her mind and body.

For fifteen minutes three or four times a day she prayed silently; her inner thoughts and feelings were as follows: "God is Love, and His Love fills my soul. God is Peace, and His Peace fills my mind and body. God is Perfect Health, and His Health is my Health. God is Joy, and His Joy is my Joy, and I feel wonderful." This kind of inner speech which represented her inner thoughts of God and His qualities brought about a complete sense of balance, poise, and harmony to her mind and body. When the thoughts of the other woman came to her mind, she would immediately identify with her aim—God's Peace. She discovered the wonders of real inner speech where her lips and heart united in identifying with the Eternal Truths of God, thereby rendering her impermeable to the impact of negative ideas and thoughts.

How do you meet people in your mind? That is the acid test for the Truth which sets you free. If you meet them and see the God in them, that is wonderful, then you are practicing the wonders of inner speech from a constructive standpoint because you are identifying with your aim, which is God or the good. Ouspensky pointed out that your inner speech should always agree with your aim.

A young man had an aim: perfect health. However, his conscious mind reminded him that he had been sick with a blood disorder for years. He was full of anxiety, fear, and doubt. His relatives kept reminding him that it would take a long time and that he might never be healed. His subconscious was, of course, receiving all these negative impressions, and he could not get a healing. His inner speech had to agree with his aim. In other words, the two phases of his mind had to synchronize and agree. This young man began to talk in a different tone to his subconscious. I told him as he listened carefully and avidly to affirm slowly, quietly, lovingly, and feelingly several times daily as follows: "The Creative Intelligence made my body and is creating my blood now. The Healing Presence knows how to heal and is transforming every cell of my body to God's pattern now. I hear and I see the doctor telling me that I am whole. I have this picture now in my mind, I see him clearly, I hear his voice, and he is saying to me, 'John, you're healed. It is a miracle!' I know this constructive imagery is going down into my subconscious mind where it is being developed and brought to pass. I know my subconscious mind is in touch with the Infinite One, and Its Wisdom and Power are bringing my request to pass in spite of all sensual evidence to the contrary. I feel this, I believe it, and I am now identifying with my aim—Perfect Health. This is my inner speech morning, noon, and night."

He repeated this prayer ten or fifteen minutes four or five times daily, particularly prior to sleep. Due to habit he found his mind running wild at times, fretting, fussing, worrying, recounting the verdict of others and his previous repeated failings in the healing

40

process. When these thoughts came to his mind, he issued the order, "Stop! I am the master. All thoughts, imagery, and responses must obey me. From now on all my thoughts are on God and His Wonderful Healing Power. This is the way I feed my subconscious. I constantly identify with God, and my inner thought and feeling is 'Thank you, Father.' I do this a hundred times a day or a thousand times, if necessary."

The young man had a healing of the blood condition in three months. This is the wonder of real and true speech wherein your inner speech is the same as it would be if you had already received the answer to your prayer. *Believe that you have it now and you shall receive.* He succeeded by repetition, prayer, and meditation to get his subconscious mind to agree with his desire; then the Creative Power of God responded according to the agreement. *Thy faith hath made thee whole.*

A woman sixty-seven years of age told me all the reasons she could not get married; then she began to silently practice correct inner speech as follows: "I thank you, Father, for my perfect, ideal, divine companion." She repeated this to herself many times a day; after a while her concept was impressed on the subconscious and she met a retired druggist whom she married. They are ideally happy. Her inner speech was one with her aim. She spoke inwardly as though it had already happened. It had happened in the only place it could ever happen, namely in her own mind.

Here is an example of wrong inner speech: A member of our organization was trying to sell a house for three years. She would decree, "I release this beautiful house to Infinite Mind. I know it is sold in Divine Order to the right person at the right price, and I give thanks now that this is so." This was her prayer and there is nothing wrong with it, but she constantly neutralized it by silently saying to herself, "Times are slow, the price is too high, people don't have that kind of money. What's wrong with me? Why can't I sell it?" You can see that she was rendering her prayer null and void.

As a man thinketh in his heart so is he. Her inner speech was very negative, and that was the way she really felt about the whole

41

matter, therefore that mental state was manifested for three years. She reversed the procedure and every night and morning she would close her eyes for five or six minutes and imagine the writer congratulating her on her sale. During the day her inner speech was: "I give thanks for the sale of my house, the buyer is prospered and blessed because of this purchase." The repetition of this phrase was impressed on her subconscious mind and made manifest. A week later a man who sat next to her in church bought her house and was very satisfied. She realized you can't go in two directions at the same time.

Let the words of my mouth, and the meditation of my heart, be acceptable in thy sight, 0 Lord, my strength, and my redeemer (Psalm 19:14)

Changing the Feeling of "I"

IF YOU SAY "I" to everything you think, feel, say, or imagine, you cannot transform your emotional life. Remember, all kinds of thoughts can enter your mind; all kinds of emotions may enter your heart. If you say "I" to all negative thoughts, you are identifying yourself with them. You can refuse to attach "I" to negative emotions and thoughts.

You naturally make it a practice to avoid muddy places as you walk along the road; likewise, you must avoid walking down the muddy roads of your mind where fear, resentment, hostility, and ill-will lurk and move. Refuse to listen to negative remarks. Do not touch the negative moods, nor let them touch you. Practice inner separation by getting a new feeling about yourself and about what you really are. Begin to realize that the real "I" in you is the Infinite Spirit, the Infinite One. Begin to identify yourself with the qualities and attributes of this Infinite One; then your whole life will be transformed.

The whole secret in transforming your negative emotional nature is to practice self-observation. To observe, and specifically to *observe oneself,* are two different things. When you say, "I observe," you mean you give your attention to external things. In self-observation the attention is directed inwards.

A man may spend his whole lifetime studying the atom, stars, body, and the phenomenalistic, external world. This knowledge cannot bring about an interior change—the change of the heart.

You must learn to differentiate, to discern, to separate the chaff from the wheat. You practice the art of self-observation when you begin to ask yourself, "Is this idea true? Will it bless, heal, and inspire me? Will it give me peace of mind as well as contribute to the general well-being of humanity?"

You are living in two worlds: the external and the internal; yet they are both one. One is visible and the other invisible (objective and subjective). Your external world enters through your five senses and is shared by everyone. Your internal world of thought, feelings, sensations, beliefs, and reaction is invisible and belongs to you.

Ask yourself, "In which world do I live? Do I live only in the world revealed by my five senses or in this inner world?" It is in this inner world you live all the time; this is where you feel and suffer.

Suppose you are invited to a banquet. All you see, hear, taste, smell, and touch belongs to the external world. All that you think, feel, like, and dislike belongs to the inner world. You attend two banquets recorded differently, namely one the outer and one the inner. It is in your inner world of thought, feeling, and emotion that you rise and fall and sway to and fro.

In order to transform yourself, you must begin to change the inner world through the purification of the emotions and the correct ordering of the mind through right thinking. If you want to grow spiritually, you must transform yourself.

Transformation means the changing of one thing into another. There are many well-known transformations of matter. Sugar through a process of distillation is changed into alcohol; radium slowly changes into lead; etc. The food you eat is transformed stage by stage into all substances necessary for your existence.

Your experiences coming in as impressions must be similarly transformed. Suppose, for example, you see a person you love and admire; you receive impressions about him. Suppose on the other hand you meet a person you dislike; you receive impressions also.

Your husband or daughter sitting on the couch as you read this is to you what you conceive him or her to be. In other words, impressions are received by your mind. If you were deaf, you would not hear their voices. You can change your impressions of people. To transform your impression is to transform yourself. To change your life, change your reactions to life. Do you find yourself reacting in stereotyped ways? If your reactions are negative, that is your life. Never permit your life to be a series of negative reactions to the impressions that come to you every day.

44

In order truly to observe yourself, you must see that regardless of what happens, your thoughts and feelings are fixed on the great truth implied by the question, "How is it in God and Heaven?" This will lift you up and transform all your negative thoughts and emotions. You may be inclined to say that other people are to blame because of the way they talk or act, but if what they say or do makes you negative, you are inwardly disturbed; this negative state is where you now live, move, and have your being.

You cannot afford to be negative; this mental state depletes your vitality, robs you of enthusiasm, and makes you physically and mentally ill. Do you live in the room where you are now or do you live in your thoughts, feelings, emotions, hopes, and despair? Is it not what you are feeling about your environment now that is real to you? When you say, "My name is John Jones," what do you mean? Is it not a fact that you are a product of your thinking plus the customs, traditions, and the influence of those around you as you grew up? You are really the sum total of your beliefs and opinions, plus what you have derived from your education, environmental conditioning, and the countless other influences acting upon you from the external world and entering through your external senses.

Perhaps you are now comparing yourself with others. Do you feel inferior in the presence of a person who seems to be more distinguished than you are? Suppose you are a fine pianist—when someone praises another pianist, do you feel inferior? If you have the real feeling of "I," this would not be possible; for the true feeling of "I" is the feeling of the Presence of the Infinite One in you, in Which there are no comparisons.

Ouspensky used to point out that people became upset easily because their feeling of "I" was derived from negative states of consciousness. "The feeling of 'I' " was one of his favorite expressions, and some of his ideas are incorporated in this essay.

I said to a man in our Bible class recently, "Have you observed your typical reaction to people, newspaper articles, and radio commentators? Have you noticed your usual, stereotyped behaviour?"

He replied, "No, I have not noticed these things." He was taking himself for granted and not growing spiritually. He began to think about his reactions; then he admitted that many of the articles and the commentators irritated him immensely. He had been reacting in a machine-like manner and was not disciplining himself. It makes no difference if all the writers and commentators were wrong and he alone was right; the negative emotion aroused in him is destructive; it shows lack of mental and spiritual discipline.

When you say, "I think this . . . ," "I think that . . . , I resent this . . . ," or "I dislike this . . . , " which "I" is speaking? Is it not a different "I" speaking every moment? Each "I" is completely different. One "I" in you criticizes one moment; a few minutes later another "I" speaks tenderly. Look at and learn about your different "I's" and know deep within yourself that certain "I's" will never dominate, control, or direct your thinking.

Take a good look at the "I's" you are consorting with. With what kind of people do you associate? I am referring to the people that inhabit your mind. Remember, your mind is a city; thoughts, ideas, opinions, feelings, sensations, and beliefs all dwell there. Some of the places in your mind are slums and dangerous streets; however, Jesus (your desire) is always walking down the streets of your mind in the form of your ideal, goal, and aim in life.

One of the meanings of Jesus is your desire; for your desire, when realized, is your saviour. Your aims and objectives in life are now beckoning to you; move toward them. Give your desire your attention; in other words, take a lively interest in it. Go down the streets of love, peace, joy, and goodwill in your mind; you will meet wonderful people on the way. You will find beautifully lighted streets and wonderful citizens on the better streets of your mind.

Never permit your house, which is your mind, to be full of servants which you do not have under control. When you were young, you were taught not to be with what your mother called "bad company." Now, when you begin to awaken to your inner powers, you must make it a special point that you do not go with the wrong "I's" (thoughts) within you.

Every time you are prone to get angry, critical, depressed, or irritable, think of God and Heaven, and ask yourself, "How is it in God and Heaven?" *There* is the answer to becoming the new man; this is how you become spiritually reborn or experience what is called the second birth. (The *second birth* is internal discipline and spiritual understanding.)

The saint and the sinner are in all of us; so are the murderer and the holy man; likewise are God and the world mind. Every man basically and fundamentally wants to be good, to express good, and to do good. This is "the positive" in you. If you have committed destructive acts, as, for example, if you have robbed, cheated, and defrauded others, and they condemn you and they hold you in a bad light, you can rise out of the slum of your mind to that exalted place in your own consciousness where you cease to condemn yourself; then all your accusers must still their tongues. When you cease to accuse yourself, the world will no longer accuse you; this is the power of your own consciousness; it is the God in you.

It is foolish to condemn yourself; you do not have to. It is idle to keep company with the thoughts of self-accusation. Suppose you committed acts of injustice, criminal acts, or other dastardly actions. It was not the God in you that did those things; it was not the real "I" or the Infinite One, it was the other self (the world mind) in you. This will not, of course, excuse you from your responsibility, no more so than if you put your hand in the fire, you will get burned; or if you pass a red light, you will get a ticket for a traffic violation.

The other self represents the many "I's" in you, for instance the many negative ideas and beliefs that there are powers outside your own consciousness; the belief that others can hurt you; or that the elements are unfriendly, plus the fears, superstitions, and ignorance of all kinds. Finally, prejudices, fears, and hates drive and goad you to do that which you would not otherwise do. The ideal way to change the feeling of "I" is to affix to the real "I" within you everything that is noble, wonderful, and God-like.

Begin to affirm, "I am strong. I am radiant. I am happy. I am inspired. I am illumined. I am loving. I am kind. I am

47

harmonious." Feel these states of mind, affirm them, and believe them. When you will begin to truly live in the garden of God. Whatever you affix to the "I AM" and believe, you become. The "I AM" in you is God, and there is none other. "I AM" or Life, Awareness, Pure Being, Existence, or the Real Self of you is God. It is the Only Cause. It is the Only Power making anything in the world. Honor It, live with the feeling "I AM illumined" all day long, and wonders will happen in your life. Feel you are inspired from On High, continue to live in that mental atmosphere, then you will draw out the wisdom, truth, and beauty from your deeper mind, and your whole world will be transformed by your inner contemplation of God's truths.

As you continue to change the feeling of "I" as outlined above, you will populate and illuminate all the recesses of your mind with God's eternal verities: *Fear not: for I have redeemed thee. . . . When thou passest through the rivers, they shall not overflow thee: when thou walkest through the fire, thou shalt not be burned* (Isaiah 43:1,2). This is the God-Presence which always goes before you whithersoever thou goest. Your dominant mental attitude or atmosphere is going ahead of you all the time creating the experiences you will encounter.

Keep in mind that when you pray about any specific thing, it is necessary to qualify your mind with the consciousness or *feeling of having or being that thing*. You mentally and completely reject the arguments in your mind against it, that is prayer. Qualify your consciousness with the thing you are praying for by thinking and deliberating about it with interest. Do this quietly and regularly until a conviction is reached in your consciousness. As you do this, the problem will no longer annoy you. You will maintain your mental poise, plus the feeling of: "I now feel that I am what I long to be," and as you continue to feel it, you will become it.

Here is the law: "I am that which I feel myself to be." Practice changing the feeling of "I" every day by affirming: "I am Spirit, I think, see, feel, and live as Spirit, the Presence of God." (The other self in you thinks, feels, and acts as the mass min does.) As you continue to do this, you will begin to feel that you are one with God. As the sun in the heavens redeems the earth from darkness and gloom, so too will the realization of the Presence of God in you reveal the man you always wished to be—the joyous, radiant, peaceful, prosperous, and successful man whose intellect is illumined by the Light from above.

God causes the sun to shine on all men everywhere. No man can take away the sunshine of God's Love from you. No one can place you in the prison of fear or ignorance when you know the Truth of God which sets you free.

The feeling that the "I AM" in you is God reveals to you that there is nothing to be afraid of and that you are one with Omnipotence, Omniscience, and Omnipresence. No one can steal health, peace, joy, or happiness from you. You no longer live with the many "I's" of fear, doubt, and superstition. You now live in the Divine Presence and in the consciousness of freedom.

Ask yourself, "Who is it that takes charge of me at every moment and speaks in His Name, calling Itself 'I'?" Never identify with the negatives, such as fear, prejudice, pride, arrogance, condemnation, etc. You now realize you need not go in the direction of the negative "I's." You will never again say "Yes" to any idle, negative thought, neither will you give it the sanction and signature of yourself.

Become the observer by keeping your eyes fixed on God—the real "I"—the Infinite One within you. Feel the sense of "I" on the observing side, and not in what you are observing. Feel that you are looking out through the eyes of God; therefore,

Thou art of purer eyes than to behold evil, and canst not look on iniquity   (Habakkuk   1:13).

Why Did This Happen To Me?

Remember ye not the former things, neither consider the things of old.
—Isaiah 43:18
But this one thing I do, forgetting those things which are behind, and reaching
forth unto those things which are before, I press toward the mark for the prize. .
.
—Phil. 3:13, 14

Whatsoever a man soweth, so also shall he reap. This means that if we plant thoughts of peace, harmony, health, and prosperity, we shall reap accordingly; and that if we sow thoughts of sickness, lack, strife, and contention, we shall reap these things. We must remember that our subconscious mind is like the soil; it will grow whatever type of seed we plant in the garden of our mind. We sow thoughts, biblically speaking, when we believe them wholeheartedly, and it is what we really believe deep down in our hearts that we demonstrate.

I had a friend who was bedridden with disease, and during my visit to her at a hospital in London, she said to me, "Why did this happen to me? What did I do to deserve this? Why is God angry at me? Why is God punishing me?" Her friends pointed out to me how kindhearted and deeply spiritual she was, and that she was a pillar of the church, etc.

It is true that she was an excellent person in many ways, but she believed in the reality of her sickness and that the condition was incurable. She believed that her heart was governed by laws of its own, independent of her thinking. This was her belief, so naturally she demonstrated accordingly. She changed her belief and began to realize that her body was spiritual and that when she changed her mind, she changed her body. She began to cease giving power to the sickness in her thought and prayed as follows: "The Infinite Healing Presence is flowing through me as harmony, health, peace, wholeness, and perfection. God's Healing Love indwells every cell."

50

She repeated this prayer frequently, and following her change of belief she had a wonderful healing. This woman had lived in fear of a heart attack for several years, not knowing that what we fear most comes to pass.

The law of life is the law of belief. Trouble of any kind is Nature's alarm signal that we are thinking wrongly in that direction, and nothing but a change of thought can set us free. Man is belief expressed, said Quimby, and we demonstrate what we really believe. There is a law of cause and effect operating at all times, and nothing happens to man without his mental consent and participation. You do not have to think of an accident to have it befall you.

Dr. Paul Tournier, the famous French psychiatrist, writes about a man who cut his hand with a saw and blamed the so-called accident on the fact that the wood which he was cutting was very wet. Dr. Tournier knew that there was a mental and emotional cause behind the severe cut on the man's hand. He discovered that the man was very irritated toward his employer, and that furthermore he had considerable rancor and hostility toward a former employer who had discharged him. Dr. Tournier explained to the man that when he is irritated and upset emotionally, his efforts become uncoordinated and jerky, and thus the accident had happened.

In the thirteenth chapter of Luke we read the following:

There were present at that season some that told him of the Galilaeans, whose blood Pilate had mingled with their sacrifices. And Jesus answering said unto them, Suppose ye that these Galilaeans were sinners above all the Galilaeans, because they suffered such things? I tell you, Nay, but except ye repent, ye shall all likewise perish. Or those eighteen, upon whom the tower in Siloam fell, and slew them, think ye that they were sinners above all men that dwelt in Jerusalem? I tell you, Nay, but, except ye repent, ye shall all likewise perish.

Jesus denies categorically that the victims of such calamities are worse sinners than other men, and adds *Except ye repent, ye shall likewise perish.* Misfortune, accidents, and tragedies of various kinds are signs of mental and emotional disorders that have broken out into manifestation. To repent means to think in a new way, to turn back to God and align our thoughts and mental imagery with the Infinite Life, Love, Truth, and Beauty of God, and then we become channels for the Divine.

Still your mind several times a day and affirm slowly, quietly, and lovingly, "God flows through me as harmony, health, peace, joy, wholeness, and perfection. God walks and talks in me. God's spell is always around me, and wherever I go God's Wisdom governs me in all my ways, and Divine right action prevails. All my ways are ways of pleasantness, and all my paths are peace."

As you dwell on these eternal verities, you will establish patterns of Divine Order in your subconscious mind, and since whatever you impress is expressed, you will find yourself watched over at all times by an Overshadowing Presence, your Heavenly Father, who responds to you when you call upon Him.

All of us are in the race mind, the great psychic sea of life. The race mind believes in sickness, accidents, death, misfortune, and tragedies of all kinds, and if we do not repent, i.e. if we do not do our own thinking, the race mind will do our thinking for us. Gradually the thoughts of the race mind impinging on our consciousness may reach a point of saturation and precipitate an accident, sudden illness, or calamity. The majority of people do not think, they *think* they think. You are thinking when you differentiate between that which is false and that which is true. To think is to choose. You have the capacity to say yes and no. Say *yes* to the Truth and reject everything unlike God or the Truth. If the mental instrument could not choose, you would not be an individual. You have the ability to accept and reject. *Think on whatsoever things are lovely, whatsoever things are just, whatsoever things are honest, whatsoever things are pure . . . think on these things.*

You are thinking when you know that there is an Infinite Intelligence which responds to your thoughts, and that no matter what the problem is, as you think about a Divine solution and the happy ending, you will find a subjective wisdom within you responding to you, revealing the perfect plan, and showing you the way you should go.

Some months ago a woman visited me stating that she had had an organic lesion for several years which failed to heal. She had taken all kinds of therapy including X-ray. She had prayed and sought prayer therapy from others without results. She told me, "God has it in for me. I'm a sinner, and this is why I am being punished." She also told me that she went to a man who hypnotized her, read her past, and had the effrontery and the audacity to tell her that she was a victim of karma, that she had wounded people in a former life, punishing them unjustly, and that now she was suffering and reaping her just deserts. Poignantly she asked, "Do you think this is why I can't be healed?"

All this is so much folderol and a monstrous absurdity. The above explanation compounded the misery and pain of the woman and offered no cure or solace. I explained to her an age-old Truth: that there is but one Power called God. It is the Creative Intelligence in all of us which created us. This Power becomes to us what we believe It to be. If a person thinks that God is punishing him and that he must suffer, *according to his thought and belief is it done unto him. As a man thinketh in his heart so is he.* This means that man's thoughts and feelings create his destiny. Man is what he thinks all day long, and if a man fails to think constructively, wisely, and judiciously, then someone else or the race mind will do his thinking for him and perhaps make a complete mess of his life.

If you believe that God is Infinite Goodness, Boundless Love, Absolute Harmony, and Boundless Wisdom, the God-Presence will respond accordingly by the law of reciprocal relationship, and you will find yourself blessed in countless ways. The forces of life are not evil, it depends how we use them. Atomic energy is not evil, it is good or bad depending on the way we use it. Man can use electricity to kill another or to vacuum the floor. You can use water to quench a child's thirst or to drown it. The wind which blows the ship on the rocks can also carry it to safety. The uses to which all things or objects in the world are put are determined by the thought of man. It is the mind of man which determines the use of the forces and objects in the world. Good and evil are movements in the mind of man relative to the One Power, which is whole, pure, and perfect. The Creative Force is in man. There is no power in the manifest universe except we give power to externals. This woman was seeking justification and alibis for her suffering. She was look-ing outside herself instead of realizing that the cause is always in her subconscious mind.

I asked her to tell me about her relationship with men. She confessed that she had an illicit love affair five years previously and that she felt guilty and full of remorse. This unresolved remorse was the psychic wound behind her organic lesion. She realized that God was not punishing her, but she was punishing herself by her own thoughts. The lesion was solidified thought which she could unthink. Life or God does not punish. If you burn your finger, Life proceeds to reduce the edema, gives you new skin, and restores it to wholeness. If you eat some tainted food, Life causes you to regurgitate and seeks to restore you to perfect health. The ancients said that the doctor dresses the wound, and God heals it.

The lesion and the morbid symptoms that no medical treatment or prayer therapy could heal, or had been able to cure, disappeared in a week. There is no worse suffering than a guilty conscience and certainly none more destructive. This woman had been punishing herself for five years by her destructive thinking, and when she ceased to condemn herself and began to claim that the Infinite Healing Presence was saturating her whole being and that God indwelled every cell of her body, the lesion disappeared. If you had been misusing the principle of electricity or chemistry for fifty years and you suddenly used it correctly, surely you would not say that the principle of electricity had a grudge against you because you had misused it. Likewise, no matter how long you may have used your mind in a negative and destructive manner, the minute you begin to use it the right way, right results follow. *Remember not the former things, neither consider the things of old* (Isaiah 43 :18) .

A man who came to see me some months ago was gradually losing his vision. He was attributing it to lack of vitamins, heredity factors, and pointed out that his grandfather went blind at eighty years of age. He belonged to a strange cult, and the cult leader, after reading his horoscope, said the planets were in a malefic configuration and that this was the cause of his failing vision. It is well known in psychosomatic circles today that psychic factors play a definite role in all disease. Nearsightedness can be brought on by workings of the mind. Treating the mental and emotional factors of the individual rather than the eye may reveal the basic emotional factor, the reason why the subconscious mind is selecting an ailment which tends to shut out everything except the immediate surroundings.

Dr. Flanders Dunbar states that certain emotional reactions can cause the involuntary muscles to twist the eyeball out of shape. In talking to this man, he revealed that he hated the sight of his mother-in-law who was living in his home. He was full of suppressed rage, and his emotional system which could not stand the strain any longer selected the eyes as the scapegoat. The explanation was the cure in this case. He was surprised to learn that negative emotions, if persisted in, snarl up in the subconscious mind and, being negative, must have a negative outlet. The negative commands to his subconscious mind—"I hate the sight of her," "I don't want to see her anymore"—were accepted by the deeper mind as a request which brought it to pass.

He made arrangements for his mother-in-law to live elsewhere and prayed for her by releasing her to God and wishing for her all the blessings of Heaven. His vision began to improve almost immediately, and in two weeks his eyesight was restored to normal. He knew he had forgiven his mother-in-law because he could meet her in his mind, and there was no longer any sting. He was trying to justify his failing vision by explaining it in terms of outside causes rather than his own mind.

A deficiency of Vitamin A can cause ophthalmia, which is an inflammation of the conjunctiva or of the eyeball, nevertheless, this could be due to ignorance, indifference, or negligence on the part of the individual. The cause in this case would be stupidity or carelessness, and the latter is a state of mind or simply a lack of knowledge. Vitamin A is omnipresent and we should have the intelligence to use it.

You cannot dodge or circumvent the law of mind. It is done unto you as you believe, and a belief is a thought in the mind. No external power or evil entity is trying to lure or harm you. People are constantly attributing their ailments to the atmosphere, the weather, to malpractice, evil entities, germs, viruses, and diet. Man pollutes the air with his strange notions and false doctrines. If a man believes that by being near an electric fan he will catch cold or get a stiff neck, that belief when accepted by him becomes his master and ruler and causes him to experience a cold. This is why the Bible says, *According to your faith is it done unto you.* The fan has no power to give anyone a stiff neck; it is harmless. Your faith can be used two ways. You can have faith in an invisible virus to give you the flu, or you can have faith in the Invisible Spirit within you to flow through you as harmony, health, and peace.

Realize that God cannot be sick, and that the Spirit in you is God; what is true of God is true of you. Believe this and you will never be sick, for according to your faith (in health and happiness) *is it done unto you.* Emerson said, "He [man] thinks his fate alien because the copula is hidden. But the soul contains the event that shall befall it; for the event is only the actualization of its thoughts, and what we pray to ourselves for is always granted. The event is the print of your form. It fits you like your skin" (from Emerson's essay "Fate").

The Devil in the Bible means ignorance or misunderstanding. Spell *live* backward and you have *evil.* Your evil is an inversion of the Life-Principle, which is God. God moves as a unity and seeks to express Himself through you as beauty, love, joy, peace, and Divine Order. The false idea in your mind is called the adversary, devil, Satan, etc. The devils which bedevil man are enmity, strife, hatred, revenge, hostility, self-condemnation, and other negative emotions. If man fails to believe in the goodness of God and in a God of Love, the extent to which he disbelieves can well be his so-called devil, which is the source of his pains, aches, and misfortunes.

A woman wrote me stating that her daughter was watching a group of men fighting on the streets of New York and that a bullet hit her daughter, necessitating the amputation of two fingers—and what was the cause of it? Was it God's will? Was it punishment for hat the accident occurred? The answer is in the negative questions of the mother. God does not judge or punish; are the movements of man's own mind. It is very ⌐king to believe that God is punishing us or that a devₐ ⌐mpting us. Our state of consciousness is always made manifest. Men, women, and children are constantly testifying to our state of consciousness. Our state of consciousness is always cause.

We do not know the contents of this girl's mind. If she was hateful, resentful, or full of hostility and self-condemnation, she could have attracted such a condition to herself. We must remember that the majority of people do not discipline, control, or direct their thinking and mental imagery along God-like channels; therefore, their failure to think constructively and harmoniously from the standpoint of the Infinite One means that they leave their minds open to the irrational mass mind, which is full of fears, hates, jealousies, and all kinds of negative happenings.

Man's failure to think the right way is as bad as thinking negatively and destructively. I remember a farmer in Ireland who waited behind a fence every day for over a week in order to shoot the landlord when he passed by. One day he was going behind the usual fence, when he stumbled, the rifle went off, and he was shot fatally. I did not understand the reason at that time, and like others, I believed it to be an accident. There are no accidents; there is a mind, a mood, a feeling behind that car, train, bicycle, and also behind the gun. This man had murder in his heart for a long time, and his subconscious responded accordingly.

No manifestation cometh unto me, save I the Father draw it. The father is your state of consciousness, your own creative power, and no experience comes to you except there is an affinity in your own mind. Two unlike things repel each other. If you walk and talk with God and believe that God is guiding you and that the Law of Harmony is always governing you, then you cannot be on a train that is wrecked because discord and harmony do not dwell together. The mother added in her letter as a postscript, "My daughter cannot get her fingers back through prayer." I don't know why people are so determined and categorical in their statements that a man cannot grow a leg or finger if missing.

Let me quote from *He Heals To-Day*, by Elsie Salmon: "Mildred was three years old when brought to me. She was born without a left hand. The arm ended in a point no bigger than the size of an index finger well above the wrist. Within a month the point at the end of the deformed arm had doubled in size and was quite plump, whereupon the father, now seeing this remarkable development, said, 'Anything can happen.' The following month there was a formation which looked like a thumb and which, at the time, we thought was a thumb. About three months following we found that this was not a thumb at all but that the growth was the whole hand at the end of the arm, and this was unfolding like a flower before our eyes."

She concludes by saying that those who were skeptical are now accepting it as an established fact. Perhaps we should take a lesson from the rhinoceros. When you take off his horns and cut out the roots, he grows new horns. Cut the legs off a crab, and he grows new legs. If a man believed he could grow a new finger, leg, or any organ, he could experience his belief.

Let us cease blaming others, let us look within for the cause of all. Believe in God, in the goodness of God, in the love of God, and in God's guidance, and you will find that all your ways will be those of pleasantness, and all your paths will be paths of peace. You are belief expressed.

How to Pray with a Deck of Cards

No ONE ACTUALLY KNOWS the real origin of the mysterious and fascinating modern playing cards. There is an old legend about the origin of cards which relates that many thousands of years ago the Chinese sages gathered together under the leadership of a great sage to discuss the fact that vast legions of brutal invaders were pillaging and plundering the land. The question to be resolved was, "How shall we preserve the ancient wisdom from the destruction of the invaders?"

There were many suggestions: Some thought that the ancient scrolls and symbols should be buried in the Himalayan Mountains. Others suggested that the wisdom be deposited in monasteries in Tibet. Still others pointed out that the sacred temples of India were the ideal places for the preservation of the wisdom of their God.

The chief sage was silent during the entire discussion, in fact he went to sleep in the midst of their_ talk, and snored loudly, much to their dismay! He awakened in a little while, and said, "Tao [God] gave me the answer, and it is this: We will order the great pictorial artists of China—men gifted with Divine imagination (which is the workshop of God)—and tell them what we wish to accomplish. We will initiate them into the mysteries of Truth. They will portray or depict in picture form the great truths which shall be preserved for all time and for countless generations yet unborn. When they are finished with the dramatization of the great Truths, Powers, Qualities, and Attributes of God through a series of picture cards, we will tell the world about a new game that has been originated. Men throughout the world for all time will use them as a game of chance, not knowing that through this simple device they are preserving the sacred teaching for all generations." This was the origin of our own deck of cards.

Many research scholars are of the opinion that cards originated in Egypt, from which the name Gypsies is derived, a nomadic tribe who travel all over the face of the earth telling fortunes and divining by cards, etc. Whether they originated in China, India, or Egypt really does not matter; the point is that they represent deep and profound psychological and spiritual truths. It is generally agreed that our cards, a composite design, are derived form the ancient Tarot cards, believed to be devised by Hebrew mystics to portray symbolically how the Laws of God work in the cosmos and in man. They consist of wands, cups, swords, and pentacles, and twenty-two of the seventy-eight Tarot cards are called "trump" cards. There is a Hebrew letter or word attached to each card, which letter has a definite, specific meaning.

You can understand the inner meaning of the Bible by a knowledge of the Hebrew alphabet and the science of symbolism. The ancients said that if all the Bibles of the world were destroyed, the Eternal Verities and the Laws of Life could be resurrected through the pictorial imagery and symbolism of the Tarot cards, from which our own cards are derived. The cards have been misused down through the ages for purposes of divination, but undoubtedly the original purpose of the cards was to convey deep and profound mystical truths to man. Divination by various means has gone on through the ages. Moses expelled haruspices, purification augurs, and those who put faith in sounds and voices. When we give heed and attention to the prophecies of evil, we are actually rejecting the First CauseGod—the Spirit within.

We must give supreme authority and recognition to the God-Presence within and become the true prophet, i.e. prophesy only the good. Our mood, our inner feeling and conviction of God's Presence and His Eternal Goodness will be made manifest in our world. Our moods and beliefs are our prophets. What we feel on the inside as true, we experience on the outside. If we start with God and realize that He rules supreme in our minds, there can be only one result—good—for God and Good are synonymous. The beginning and the end are always the same. Begin with God as Supreme Power and Boundless Love, and you will always be certain of the future. The future is always the present grown up. It is your thought made visible. You can be absolutely certain of your future if you will now, today, plant whatsoever things are true, lovely, noble, and God-like in the Garden of God—your own mind.

You mold, fashion, shape, and direct your own destiny. The future is already in your mind and may be changed by prayer, meditation, and mystic visioning. You can be brainwashed and hypnotized by others into believing their dire predictions of misfortune and loss, but you must remember you abdicated your authority and permitted your thoughts to move negatively, creating the thing you feared. "What I feared most has come upon me" (Job).

The minute you set up a rival to God in your mind, you are looking for trouble and asking for trouble. Your faith in God and His Love is your good fortune, and from now on you believe and live in the constant expectancy of the best. What is true of God is true of you. It is wonderful!

DESCRIPTION OF THE CONTEMPORARY DECK OF CARDS

THERE ARE FIFTY-TWO playing cards and two extra cards called the "Jokers," and they are enclosed in a cover and sealed. It is necessary to break the seal to use the cards. This is symbolic of man, for every man is a book which is sealed. Man houses God—he is the tabernacle of the Living God, for God's tabernacle is with man. Within man is the God-Presence. All the Intelligence, Wisdom, and Power of the Infinite One are located in the depths of man, waiting to be resurrected. Man must break the seal and learn of the imprisoned splendour within. When man learns of the powers of his conscious and subconscious mind and the law of action and reaction, he has broken the seal and is beginning to realize that thoughts are things—that what he feels, he attracts, and that what he believes, he experiences. If you think in a certain way repeatedly, you form an impression or concept in the subconscious area of your mind which becomes a subconscious force governing your outer actions.

Man unveiled is Spirit, Mind. When you think of yourself apart from your body, your name, your nationality, home, and environment, what are you? Divest yourself now of your body, and you will say, "I am Spirit, I am Mind." You are mentally disrobing yourself or breaking the seal, and you find the Kingdom of God is within.

The Joker is the odd card and is usually rejected but, of course, is given greater value when used in playing a game. The joker is God, and He is usually rejected by man, because the average man has a God outside himself—a sort of anthropomorphic being living in the skies, a punishing, avenging Deity—or he has a vague, confused concept of God which is based on ignorance, fear, and superstition. The average man rejects the Joker or the Indwelling God, he refutes the fact that his own consciousness is God to his world, and that he creates and fashions his own future by his thoughts and feelings.

When you use the Joker or the Hidden Power within, it magnifies everything in your life. Begin to use the Divine Power within you, and magnify your health, peace, happiness, and joy: this is the meaning of the Joker. We can't afford to neglect the Spiritual Power within. If we do not pray, meditate, commune with God, and imbibe His Truths, we get immersed in the negative atmosphere of the world, such as fear, war, rumors of war, man's inhumanity to man, business problems, newspaper headlines, etc. If we continue to feed mentally on all sorts of troubles, sicknesses, calamities, all these thoughts reach a point of fulfillment within us, resulting in the precipitation of sickness, disease, and all sorts of disorder in our lives.

It does not pay to reject the Stone of Truth. "The Stone which the builders rejected is made head of the corner." Put God back on the throne of your mind, claim His Guidance and Direction, and become replenished from the standpoint of Truth and Beauty.

There are fifty-two cards, which, when added together, form the numeral 7. There are fifty-two weeks in the year, which represents the end of a solar cycle. The cycle also takes place in our own mind. When you entertain an idea, nourish it mentally, and become absorbed in the reality of it, the idea passes from your conscious mind to your subconscious, and the cycle is completed, because you have impressed your subconscious with your concept, idea, plan, or purpose. Whatever is impressed in the subconscious will be expressed, and your cycle is completed When impregnation of the subconscious mind takes place, it is called the "sixth day"; that is, your mental and emotional act is completed. This is followed by a rest, called the "seventh day," or the day of rest in God. There is always an interval of time between the impregnation of the subconscious and the external manifestation of your prayer. This period of time is referred to as the Sabbath, or inner certitude, which follows the joy of the answered prayer. The Sabbath Day is more fully explained in my book *Peace within Yourself.* [1]

The pack consists of four suits: Clubs, Hearts, Spades, and Diamonds, symbolizing the spiritual, mental, emotional, and physical nature of man. The four suits represent also the four letters in the name Jehovah, which are Yod-He-Vau-He. "Yod" means I Am, or God, the Spirit within. "He" is your desire or mental picture. "Vau" means nail, or feeling; and the final "He" is the external manifestation of what you saw and felt within as true in your own mind. In simple, everyday language, all it means is that whatever the idea, concept, or mental image you entertain in your mind, if you feel it and acknowledge it, you shall experience the result, whether it be negative or positive.

The four suits of cards are telling you how to pray, for that is the way you bring all experiences, conditions, and events into your life. It is the way all things are made manifest in your world, and there is nothing experienced by you that is not made that way.

EACH SUIT: THIRTEEN CARDS

Three of each suit are picture cards, namely King, Queen, and Jack, and ten are spot cards, from Ace (or one) to ten inclusive. The King, Queen, and Jack refer to the Trinity—the Father, Mother, and Child—which is represented symbolically in all the

* Published by DeVorss & Company

great religions of the world. In simple, everyday language, the idea or thought you have is the father, feeling is the mother, and the union of the two brings forth issue or a mental child, which could be a healing of the mind, body, pocketbook, or business problem. The simple answer as well as the simple prayer is always the best.

Another explanation of the King card is that you were born to be a King over your own mind, body, and circumstances. The illumined, conscious mind is King, for it orders, directs, and issues instructions to the Queen, the subconscious or subjective, feeling nature. The Jack represents your purified desire, idea, or plan not yet made manifest. There must, therefore, be a synchronous union of the conscious and subconscious mind with your desire, and if both are in agreement, it shall come to pass and nothing shall be impossible unto you.

There are ten spot cards. I shall explain the numeral 10 briefly: 1 represents the male, and 0 represents the female. The union of the two results in the creative act, mentally and spiritually speaking as well as physically. The ten spot cards represent the harmonious interaction of your conscious and subconscious mind along all four phases of your life—spiritual, mental, emotional, and material. The virtues of ten are infinite in number. The numeral 10 means God in infinite differentiation, because you can add countless zeros to the numeral 1.

THE PICTURE CARDS

These cards are double, indicating our dual nature; we are living in a mental and spiritual world and also in an objective or three-dimensional world. When the outside world displeases us, we can go to the realm of mind, pray, and identify with our ideal by nourishing it, and through frequent occupancy of the mind we will bring it to pass; then the outside and the inside become one, and we are at peace. We change the outside by changing the inside. The outer is always a reflection of the inner. "As within, so without." There are two ends to the stick, there is an inside and an outside to everything. Life is a Oneness functioning as duality; there is night and day, ebb and flow, male and female, hot and cold, peace and pain, health and sickness, objective and subjective, invisible and visible, positive and negative, matter and spirit, good and evil. The opposites are dual expressions of the same eternal principle, which is forever whole and perfect in Itself.

THE HEADDRESS

The kings wear beards, which symbolize Wisdom and the Power of God. The crowns portray authority and the regency of Spirit ruling in the mind of man. The King of Diamonds with hand uplifted indicates his allegiance to God—the One Power—and behind him is an axe, suggesting that the law of the subconscious is always exact, mathematical, and just. "As we sow so also shall we reap." The axe also is indicative of the negative reaction of the law if we violate the law of harmony or Divine order in our life. Think evil, evil follows; think good, good follows—that is the law. The King of Hearts with the sword in his hand indicates the sword of Truth. "Think not that I am come to send peace on earth; I come not to send peace, but a sword" (Matthew 10:34).

Truth comes into your mind to divide it and separate the debris from the Truths of God. Truth separates you from the old, false beliefs of the race, provoking an inner quarrel, thereby resolving all differences and enthroning peace in the heart. The King of Hearts has pierced his heart (subconscious mind) with the Eternal Truths. The three swords held respectively by the King of Clubs, King of Spades, and King of Hearts possess sheaths which allude to holding the torch of Truth aloft in all phases of our life—mental, emotional, and physical.

Clubs represent your thoughts and ideas, Hearts your feeling or emotional nature, Spades your deep conviction where you dig or implant ideas in your subconscious, and Diamonds the world, the external objectification of your internal thoughts, feelings, and beliefs. In other words, you have the story of prayer given to you in many ways in a deck of cards. When you look at the four Queens in your cards, you will notice they hold a flower, the symbol of purity, love, beauty, order, symmetry, and proportion. The heart is the chalice of God's love and Beauty, which is to remind us that we should fill our hearts with God's Love, and the flowers of beauty, peace, joy, and happiness will appear on the earth—our world.

The Queen of Spades (the dominant feeling in your subconscious) holds a torch in her hand. This is the Light that lighteth every man that cometh into the world. It is to remind you that the Infinite Intelligence of God is within your subconscious depths, and that by that Light you can walk through darkness. When your sense evidence tells you something is impossible, you see by an inner Light, your eyes are on the solution which the God-Wisdom will bring to you as you hold your faith in God aloft. Let this torch be a candle which forever shines upon your head.

The Jack of Spades holds an hourglass, indicating that we are moving through time and space on this three-dimensional plane, and that whatever idea you have conveyed to the subconscious will come forth in its own way and its own time, because its ways are past finding out. The ways of the subconscious are not your ways, and you do not know the hour or the day—that is the secret of your subconscious self. The feather held by the Jack of Hearts and the axe behind his head tell you symbolically of the Law and the Word—the feather is your concept or idea, and the law executes it. Make sure your plan conforms to the good of all, and that it hurts no one. When in trouble, think of God and His answer. He knows only the answer—this is the "feather's weight" that saves you.

The robes and vestments worn by the figures are beautiful, elegant, and colorful—they indicate the seven colors of the solar spectrum. White is the purity, wholeness, and perfection of God. White is called the mother of all colors. The colors on the cards tell us of the immaculate and unblemished Presence within us. Red indicates purified desire and divinity. Scarlet stands for enthusiasm and God-Intoxication. Purple indicates royalty, or God's Wisdom reigning supreme in our mind. Green stands for God's abundance and fruitful ideas and thoughts. Blue indicates the subconscious area of our mind or the Law of God. Yellow indicates the Power, Strength, and Glory of the Infinite One.

NUMBER OF CARDS IN EACH SUIT

There are thirteen cards in each suit to remind us of our twelve powers, twelve faculties. You and your twelve powers are symbolized by the number 13. It behooves us all to develop and discipline these powers, so that a God-like man appears on the earth who will unstop the ears of the deaf, open the eyes of the blind, and do all the things a son of God should do.

You have forty spot cards. Noah was forty days in the ark, Jesus fasted for forty days—all these stories are symbolic of the fast from the poisoned feast of race thoughts and false concepts, as well as of our mental absorption in the good we seek to bring to pass. The length of time it takes you to detach yourself from your problem and reach a conviction in your mind is called forty days, or the completion of a cycle of consciousness. Fast from poverty thoughts and feast on God's Abundance—reject the appearance of things, the verdict or opinion of others, and give all your attention to the idea of God's Opulence. Gradually you qualify your consciousness, whether it takes an hour, a week, or a month. Sooner or later you will succeed in impregnating your subconscious with the idea of wealth. You have fasted for forty days, and you will experience God's wealth in your world.

The rods held by the Jack of Clubs and the jack of Diamonds indicate a measuring rod or the cubit. *Man* means mind or measurer. You are to measure and appropriate in your mind the Infinite Goodness and Love of God, for your concept of God is your concept of yourself. The idea I have is one that I must cube, and cube is "mother" in Hebrew. Mother your idea, love it, and make it alive, then you have a spiritual standard to measure all things by.

I wish to touch on the hanging leaf on the Jack of Clubs. Clubs refer to the ideas, plans, and purposes in your mind, the scheme, diagram, or blueprint. You will notice on the Jack of Clubs how he bows over. This is humility, giving all honor and glory to God. Our attitude should be, "Father, I thank thee that thou hast heard me; and I knew that thou hearest me always" (John 11:41).

It is generally agreed that the number value, mathematical quantities, colors, and symbolism of the playing cards have a very close connection with the Great Pyramid. The ancient mystics who devised playing cards thousands of years ago knew all about the rotation of the earth on its axis and were able to measure the heavens and the earth, all of which is portrayed in the cards and the Great Pyramid. Men like Job intuitively perceived the laws written in our hearts and inscribed in our inward parts. "Where wast thou when I laid the foundations of the earth? Declare, if thou hast understanding. Who hath laid the measures thereof, if thou knowest? Or who hath stretched the line upon it? Whereupon are the foundations thereof fastened? or who laid the corner stone thereof?" (Job 38:4-6).

Write a New Name in the Book of Life

THE BOOK OF LIFE is your subconscious mind, and you are always writing in that Book of Life based on your habitual thinking and imagining. Shakespeare said, "What is in a name?" Well, when I mention your name, it indicates your particular sex, your nationality, your background, your training, your education, your financial structure, your social status, and all things appertaining to you.

Shakespeare wrote many plays. *Romeo and Juliet*, for example, is a drama of your own conscious and subconscious mind. And when your conscious and subconscious mind work harmoniously, peacefully, and joyfully together, the children of that union are happiness, peace, health, abundance, and security. The disharmonious relationship of the conscious and subconscious mind brings misery, suffering, pain, sickness, and disease into your life.

Abram left Ur of Chaldea. Ur means sorcery, black magic, worship of stars, idols, and all that sort of thing. Abram changed his name to Abraham, meaning the father of the multitude, indicating the one God, the one Presence and Power.

We are all children of the one God. That's the unity of all life. All men and women are brothers—same mind, same spirit, and same substance. Therefore to hurt another is to hurt yourself, and to bless another is to bless yourself.

You can write a new name, a new estimate, a new blueprint of yourself. Get a new concept of yourself. Is it great enough, noble enough, or grand enough to redeem you, to bring about an inner transformation of your heart, your mind, and your whole being? Today people have many idols, just as they had in Chaldea years ago. Superstition is rampant. They still have false gods, such as "The weather is going to give me a cold," or "If I wet my feet, I am

69

going to get pneumonia." Some are afraid of germs, so that when someone sneezes, they feel they may get the virus. If you ask the exposed person, "Did you get the virus this year?" the response is, "No, not yet." The infection is anticipated, though. What you expect, you always get.

Some say, "I don't know the right Congressman. I have no pull. I can't get that job." They are denying the Creative Power within them. They say It is omnipotent and supreme, yet all the time they are denying It. If It is supreme and omnipotent, there is nothing to oppose It or challenge It. Therefore you should say, "Infinite Spirit opens up the door for me, revealing to me my hidden talents and showing me the way I should go." That's exactly what the Infinite Spirit will do for you.

There are Congressmen who speak and touch wood when they talk about something negative, as if the wood had some power. Do you give power to other people? To the atmosphere? To the weather? All these things are impotent. They have no power. The power is in you.

Saul's name was changed to Paul. The meaning of Paul is the "Little Christ," and many miracles were wrought by the hand of Paul. Paul was illumined on the road to Damascus, which means a sack of blood, or rebirth. This means a mystical illumination where your mind, or intellect, is flooded with the light of God and you are a transformed man. Sometimes this takes place in the twinkling of an eye, like that which was experienced by St. Theresa and many others.

Paul became a changed man. He was no longer the murderer who sent people to death. He was transformed. He was illumined from On High. You can go to court and change your name every year if you wish. It doesn't mean anything. It is absolutely meaningless. You must change your nature, your disposition, your viewpoint, your concept of yourself. There must be an inner transformation. Then, of course, you have changed your name, or your nature.

Some time ago a man came to see me who was cynical and a sourpuss who would snarl at his secretary and at the salesman

70

when he came in. If someone said, "It's a good day," he would say, "What's good about it?" When he came down to breakfast in the morning, he would hold the paper up in front of himself lest he see his wife. He would always criticize the bacon and the eggs. He was just a plain sourpuss—nasty and ugly.

He went to a psychologist, and the psychologist said, "I'll tell you what you do. You can change your whole nature. When you come down in the morning, kiss your wife and tell her she looks lovely and that the food is delicious, and she'll probably faint." The man said, "Well, I'll be a hypocrite if I do that." The psychologist said, "Go ahead. Start it anyhow. Break the ice in your heart. When you go into the office, tell the secretary how beautiful her hair is, or her eyes—there must be something lovely about her. And be genial, courteous, and affable to the salesman."

After a month's time, as he practiced these things, gradually they sank into his subconscious mind and he became transformed— genial, affable, amiable, and philosophical. People said, "What happened to that fellow?" Others said, "He's in love." Well, I guess he was—in love with the Higher Self.

"He that guided me this far will open up the rest of the way." That's a magnificent truth. A teacher wrote me from Alabama, and I gave him that simple truth. He said his building was three-quarters finished and now there was a strike; he didn't have the money, and what was he going to do? "He that guided me this far will open up the rest of the way."

He said, " 'That' is not correct. You should say, 'He *who* guided me will open up the rest of the way.' " I said, "No. I meant 'that' literally." It was not a slip. It was deliberate, because I am dealing with a Principle, an impersonal Presence which is no respecter of persons, a universal Presence and Power available to all men. The cutthroat, beggar, thief, holy man, atheist or agnostic—any man can tap it. Any man can use it.

God is not a person, so we don't say, "Our Father *who* art in Heaven." We say, "Our Father *which* art in Heaven, indicating an impersonal Presence and Power—an Infinite Life and Infinite

Intelligence. So, you see, he had a concept of a God-man up in the sky somewhere. He practiced, however, what I taught him to do, and he found that he attracted the necessary funds to complete the building.

This Universal Presence creates out of Itself by means of Its becoming that particular thing. In other words, God becomes man by believing Himself to be man. God creates a being out of Himself capable of returning glory, light and love to Himself. Abraham knew the Creative Power. He was aware of it, and he demonstrated It in his life. He believed that the Spirit would guide and direct him, which, of course, It did.

PLATO, ARISTOTLE, PLOTINUS, ETC., ALL SPOKE OF GOD AS INFINITE

Mind and Infinite Intelligence, but they didn't tell you how to use the Presence and Power for guidance, for harmony, for prosperity, for success, or how to heal yourself with It. It was a satisfactory intellectual conclusion—very interesting. But they didn't tell you how to use It in everyday practice.

If you believe you are an old worm of the dust, people will step on you and will treat you the way you treat yourself. If you are cruel and nasty to yourself, the world will be cruel and nasty to you. As within, so without. Realize you are a son or a daughter of the Living God. You are heir to all of God's riches. Realize you should exalt God in the midst of you mighty to heal. How could you feel inferior if you knew that you are a daughter of the Infinite, that you are a darling of God, and that God loves you and cares for you? God is the Life Principle, or the Living Spirit within you, which created you and watches over you when you are sound asleep, because He who watches over you neither slumbers nor sleeps.

There are a great many people who work very hard, but they nevertheless fail in life. The reason is that they have a subconscious pattern of failure, or they believe they should fail. Sometimes they think a jinx is following them. They feel inferior. Perhaps they were told when they were young, "You'll never amount to anything.

You'll always be a failure. You are stupid. You are dumb." These thoughts were accepted by their impressionable mind and now these thoughts have a life of their own in the subconscious mind, and are experienced by them.

But man can change his life. These subconscious or irrational impulses act long after the events which caused them have been forgotten. Man can feed the subconscious mind with something new. He can say, "I'm born to succeed, the Infinite cannot fail." He can feed his subconscious such life-giving patterns as: "Divine law and order govern my life; Divine peace fills my soul; Divine love saturates my mind; Divine right action reigns supreme; Infinite Intelligence guides and directs me in all my ways—It is a lamp unto my feet and a light upon my path."

When you are angry, suspicious, or full of fear, these emotions are negative and destructive. They snarl up in the subconscious mind, and they cause you to do the wrong thing and to say the wrong thing. When you want to be happy, you're sad; when you want to do the right thing, you do the wrong thing. This is true when you are under the sway of negative and destructive emotions, for whatever you do then will be wrong.

So you can write a new name in the Book of Life. The Book of Life, as we explained to you, is the law of your own subconscious. The Bible says, I saw in the right hand of Him that sat on the throne a book written within and on the backside, sealed with seven seals. And I saw a strong angel proclaiming with a loud voice, Who is worthy to open the book, and to loose the seals thereof? And no man in heaven, nor in earth, neither under the earth, was able to open the book, neither to look thereon. And I wept much, because no man was found worthy to open and to read the book, neither to look thereon (Revelation 5:1-4).

Now the book written within and on the backside is your objective and subjective mind. You have a conscious and subconscious mind. Whatever thoughts, beliefs, opinions, theories, or dogmas you write, engrave, or impress on your subconscious mind you experience as objective manifestations—as circumstances, conditions, and events. What we write on the inside we experience on the outside. We have two sides of our lives—objective and subjective, visible and invisible, thought and its manifestation.

The seven seals are the seven states of consciousness. Our concept passes through seven degrees of awareness whereby we spiritualize our five senses by turning inward to the Spiritual Power. Then we get our conscious and subconscious mind to agree and synchronize. When there is no longer any doubt in your conscious or subconscious mind, your prayer is always answered. You break the seven seals when you discipline your five senses and get the two phases of your mind to agree.

There are seven seals. The first is sight. This means to see the truth about any situation. See perfect health where sickness is; see harmony where discord is; love where hatred is. Then you are seeing the truth, and you are disciplining your faculty of sight.

The second is hearing. You hear the glad tidings, the truths of God. You hear your mother tell you what you long to hear—that the miracle of God has happened; that she is healed. In other words, you don't see her in a hospital as being ill. You hear the opposite. You hear her tell you about her perfect health. Then you are hearing the truth.

The third is smell. You smell the truth by coming to a definite decision, realizing that God who made your body can also heal it. You reject all other "food" as unfit for mental consumption. A dog smells food; if it is unsavory, he rejects it. Likewise, reject all thoughts, ideas, and opinions that do not fill your soul with joy.

The fourth is taste. You taste the sweet savor of God. You taste the truth by appropriating the ideas or truths of God in your mind through meditation and through frequent occupancy of the mind regarding the perfect outcome you want.

The fifth is the joy when you touch mentally and emotionally the answered prayer, while feeling the reality of it.

The remaining two seals are your conscious and subconscious mind. When you succeed in disciplining the five senses, the male and female principles in your own mind begin to interact harmoniously. A Divine marriage takes place between your desire and your emotion, and a child comes forth from the union, which is the joy of the answered prayer.

That's the Book of Life that people are talking about. If someone should photograph your subconscious mind, they could see your future, your past, and your present thinking. The future is your present thoughts grown up. You can always change the future by changing the present. Feast on whatsoever things are true, lovely, noble, and God-like. Think these thoughts with conviction. The old thoughts will die. They'll fade away. They'll be obliterated, expunged from your deep mind, because the lower is subject to the higher.

Think of everything lovely and of good report. Get new thoughts, new ideas, regarding principles and the eternal verities. Remember, your subconscious mind does not accept your idle wishes, dreams or hopes. It accepts your convictions—what you really believe deep down in your heart.

What do you believe? Do you believe in the goodness of God in the land of the living, and the guidance of God, and the harmony of God, and the love of God, and the abundance of God? If you do, all these things will come to pass because to believe is to live in the state of what is believed in. It's to accept something as true.

Look at your spiritual heritage. We are all children of the I AM, as Moses says. Within you is the real nature or the real name, because you are pronouncing it all day long. I AM. It's called Om in India. The Bible says, *I AM THAT I AM* (Exodus 3:14). Moses said, *I AM hath sent me unto you* (Exodus 3:14).

Realize I AM sends you to your business tomorrow, to a tough assignment, to solve it, to overcome it. The engineer, when he meets with a pressing problem, realizes I AM has sent him there to solve the problem. The engineer grapples with the problem courageously, and he sees the solution.

We are all children of the I AM (God). Whatever you attach to I AM, you become. If you say, I am no good, I'm a flop, I'm a failure, I'm going deaf, I'm going blind, I'm nobody, whatever you attach to it you become. Reverse it and say, "I am happy, joyous, and free. I am illumined, I am inspired, I am strong, I am powerful. 'Let the weak say, I am strong.' Let the widow say, it is well.' I am a son [or daughter] of the Living God. I am heir to all of God's riches. I am born to win, to succeed, for the Infinite cannot fail. I am a tremendous success. I am absolutely outstanding. I am unique, and there is no one in all the world like me."

Why don't you claim the above and write these truths in your heart and inscribe them in your inward parts? He that hath an ear, let him hear what the Spirit saith unto the churches: To him that overcometh will I give to eat of the hidden manna, and will give him a white stone, and in the stone a new name written, which no man knoweth saving he that receiveth it (Revelation 2:17).

Manna is a symbol of the bread of Heaven. *I am the living bread which came down from Heaven* (John 6:51). It's the bread of peace, of harmony, it's the blessed bread of God. Eat the bread of inspiration and guidance, for no man can live in this world today without spiritual food. You may sit down to dinner and have the choicest food but still be hungry for peace, harmony, love, inspiration, and guidance.

Manna is a symbol of inspiration, of strength, of power, and of wisdom. It will feed you in the desert of loneliness, of unhappiness, because the greatest desert of the world is not the Sahara, it's under the hat of man. There is very little growing there but weeds of ignorance, fear, and superstition. Buddha asked God the cause of all misery, suffering, crime, and sickness in the world. The answer he received was "ignorance," for ignorance is the only sin, and all punishment is the consequence.

Call on this Presence and Power. It will answer you. It will be with you in trouble. It will set you On High, because you have known Its name or nature. The nature of Infinite Intelligence is to respond to you. Turn within to the Fountain of Life and feel refreshed from the standpoint of truth. You can be replenished there. *Come ye to the waters, and he that hath no money, come ye, buy, and eat, yea, come, buy wine and milk without money and without price* (Isaiah 55:1). The price is recognition, acceptance, conviction. The price is to honor God and to believe in Him. That's the only price you pay.

If you don't honor God and recognize Him, it's just the same as if the Presence were not there. You can eat of the bread of peace, of joy, of faith, and of confidence in the only Power there is. Your confidence and faith should not be in creeds, dogma, and traditions. Believe that whatever you impress on your subconscious will be expressed as form, function, experience, and event. Then you are learning to know yourself a little better.

A new name is a new disposition, a new perspective, a new insight. You can affirm, "God loves me and cares for me. I am illumined from On High." You can claim right action. You can claim, "The wisdom of God anoints my intellect and I am now writing this with my conscious pen into my subconscious mind. Whatever I inscribe in my subconscious mind becomes effective and functional."

You are here to solve problems. The reason you have problems and challenges is that you are here to discover your Divinity and sharpen your mental and spiritual tools, otherwise you'd never discover yourself.

There are failures in life, yes! That's why you had an eraser at the end of your pencil when you went to school. Everybody knew you were going to make mistakes. Through the mistakes, however, you learned how to add and subtract as well as many, many other things.

You must have a basis for thinking constructively. When you know that thoughts are things and that what you feel you attract, and that what you imagine you become, then you begin to think constructively because you realize, "My thought is creative—not because it's my thought, but because it is thought."

"Nothing can give you peace but the triumph of principles," wrote Emerson. Quimby said that a child is like a little blank tablet, and the uncles, and the aunts, and the clergyman, and everybody else comes along and scribbles something on it. This is easy to do because the little mind, of course, is impressionable, malleable, and open to all the beliefs, opinions, creeds, dogmas, superstition, ignorance, and fear of the parents. The child grows up in the image and the likeness of the dominant mental, emotional, and spiritual climate of the home.

Who is scribbling on your mind today? Does your mother-in-law, father-in-law, or some in-law scribble something on your mind? Do they disturb you? Does someone tell you you are going to fail? Or do you reject it and say, "You don't know what you are saying. I can't fail. How could I fail? The Infinite is within me. I am born to win. I am a success in my prayer life, in my relationship with people, and in my chosen work." The minute you affirm the above, the Power will respond to you.

How could the Infinite fail? Where is the Infinite? Within you. And you are born to win, to overcome, to triumph. You are here to go from glory to glory, and from octave to octave, for there is no end to the glory which is man.

Is the columnist writing something in your mind? Or are you writing the truths of God, which are the same yesterday, today, and forever? What are you writing in your mind every day? Some people write grief, despair, hopelessness, loneliness, etc. Inscribe the conviction that you are worthy, that you are adequate, that you are full of faith and confidence in the only Power there is, and that you know you are inspired from On High, and you believe implicitly that God is guiding you in all your ways and is a Lamp unto your feet and a Light upon your path.

Your subconscious mind, which is the Book of Life, will receive these impressions, viewpoints, opinions, and convictions because you are sincere, because you mean them. Whatever you think, feel, and believe to be true, your subconscious mind will bring to pass— good or bad.

Inscribe in your mind harmony, health, wholeness, beauty, peace, perfection, and right action. These are principles. You do not create these truths, but you activate them and make them effective and functional when you affirm them. Stir up the gifts of God within you.

Anything that fills you with faith, with confidence, with joy, and with enthusiasm has power over you, and it governs your conduct. Enthusiasm governs all your activities, because enthusiasm means "possessed by God." You will never go so far as when you are possessed by the One—the Beautiful and the Good.

You are a mental and a spiritual being, because when you say I AM, you are announcing the Presence of the Living God. You have always lived. A billion years from now you will be alive, because Life was never born and will never die; water wets it not, fire burns it not, wind blows it not away. You are alive, and that life is God's life. God is Life; therefore, you have always lived.

Are you the same person you were five years ago? Ten years ago? Twenty-five years ago? No, you're not. Are you the same person you were when you were three months old or a year old? You have had hundreds of reincarnations since you were born. Reincarnation is Spirit making Itself manifest at higher levels. So, at five years of age you were different, at 10, at 20, and at 30. If I showed you photographs of every month of your life, you would hardly recognize yourself in some of them.

You are not the same as you were six months ago. You have a new concept of God, of Life, of the universe—a new estimate, a new blueprint, a new insight. You don't talk the same; you don't walk the same or think the same. Your life is going from glory to glory. When you go on to the next dimension, you still go on from octave to octave. You can't be less tomorrow than you are today, for life goes not backward nor tarries with yesterday.

Write, "I go from glory to glory. I go from octave to octave." Write these truths in your life, because you are alive and you are always implanting something new in your deeper mind.

I receive many letters, a few of which say, "You will be cast into a lake of fire because you are telling people on your radio program that each man is his own saviour, that God indwells him, and that all he has to do is contact this God-Presence and It will lead him, guide him, and solve his problems for him. You also say that every man answers his own prayers. Some day you

will burn in the lake of fire for all eternity for saying these things." Then they quote the Bible and say, *"For God so loved* the world, that He gave his only begotten Son, that whosoever believeth in him should not perish, but have everlasting life" (John 3:16).

All this is based on a lack of understanding. Everybody is the only begotten Son. We are all begotten of the Only One. There is only One. Your only begotten Son, spiritually speaking, is

your desire. If you are sick, health is your savior. You have a desire for health. Realization of your desire is your savior. If you are lost in the woods, guidance is your savior. If you are imprisoned, freedom is your savior. If you are dying of thirst, water is your savior. So every man who is able to contact the God-Presence is, of course, his own savior.

The lake of fire mentioned in the Bible is no literal fire, of course. The Bible is a spiritual book. It is speaking in spiritual, mental, allegorical, figurative, idiomatic, and mystical language. When you go to a hospital in the psychotic ward, or in any mental institution, you will find people there burning in the lake of fire. The lake, of course, is your subconscious mind. The fire means they are seething with jealousy, hate, resentment, hostility, and anger. They are burning up their tissues and their hearts with these negative emotions.

A psychotic is tormented, isn't he? He's on fire with his own misery. Some people are on fire with their own hatred, resentment, hostility, etc. Of course, they are living in a lake of fire created by themselves, because every man creates his own hell and his own heaven. Omar said:

I sent my Soul through the Invisible,
Some letter of that After-Life to spell:
And by and by my Soul return'd to me,
And answer'd "I Myself am Heav'n and Hell. "

Anger, depression, fear, and foreboding are the inner fires. The doctor tells you these emotions give you ulcers, high blood pressure, cancer, and arthritis. Hate will give you arthritis if you keep it up; it will bring about changes, bring on calcareous deposits in your tissues, and play havoc with you. Sometimes jealousy will drive a person absolutely insane, because there is no more destructive poison than jealousy. It is called the green-eyed monster and is the greatest of all mental poisons.

Therefore sow for yourself treasures in heaven, where the moth and the rust do not consume, and where thieves cannot break through and steal. Sow for yourself harmony, health, peace, and beauty. Write in your heart the truths of God. What will you write? Write . . . whatsoever things are true, whatsoever things are honest, whatsoever things are just, whatsoever things are pure, whatsoever things are lovely, and whatsoever things are of good report. If there be any virtue, if there be any praise, think on these things now and forever more (Philippians 4:8).

The Song of Triumph
Tell me, O thou whom my soul loveth, where thou feedest,
where thou makest thy flock to rest at noon?
Behold, thou art fair, my love; behold, thou art fair, thou hast doves' eyes.
He brought me to the banqueting house, and his banner over me was love.
His left hand is under my head, and his right hand doth embrace me.
My beloved spake, and said unto me,
Rise up, my love, my fair one, and come away.
For lo, the winter is past, the rain is over and gone;
The flowers appear on the earth; the time of the singing of
birds is come, and the voice of the turtledove is heard in our land;
Arise, my love, my fair one, and come away.
My beloved is mine, and I am his; he feedeth among the lilies.
Until the day break, and the shadows flee away.
—*The Song of Solomon*

IT IS INCONCEIVABLE that any anthology could be written wherein The Song of Solomon was not included. It is really one of the most inspired parts of the Bible. The Song of Solomon reveals God as Universal love. It is ecstatic and thrilling.

In order to lead the triumphant life, you must be moved by love. You can go wild in the joy of being intoxicated by the Spirit. In other words, by singing the song of triumph you become God-intoxicated and fired with Divine enthusiasm, thereby expressing more and more of Divine love and joy every day.

You sing the song of God, or the mood of triumph, when you subjectively feel that you are that which your five senses tell you you are not, you are then God-intoxicated and seized with a Divine frenzy—a sort of mad joy.

Haven't you at times seen a person bubbling over with enthusiasm and apparently intoxicated with joy? That person was singing the Song of God at that moment. *In thy presence is fulness of joy; at thy right hand there are pleasures for evermore* (Psalm 16:11).

When you give voice to a song, you are expressing your whole nature. Your mind and body enter into the song. When your heart is full of love and goodwill, and you are radiating peace, you are truly singing God's Song; it is the song of the jubilant soul.

The real You is a spiritual, eternal, perfect being. You are a living expression of God now. *I have said, Ye are gods; and all of you are children of the most High* (Psalm 82:6).

When you pray, it is a romance with God or your Good. Your desire, when realized, brings you joy and peace. In order to realize the desire of your heart, which is depicted in The Song of Solomon as your beloved, you must woo it; let that desire of yours captivate, hold, and thrill you. Let it fire your imagination. You will always move in the direction of the desire which dominates your mind.

The majority of students of Divine Science know that The Song of Solomon is a beautiful description of the harmonious union of the conscious and subconscious mind (Solomon and Sheba).

"Tell me, O thou whom my soul loveth, where thou feedest." Your realized desire is he whom your soul loveth. You are asked "where thou feedest." In other words, what are you mentally dwelling upon? The *flock* represents your thoughts, ideas, opinions, and beliefs. You are to feast on nothing but the joy of the answered prayer.

If you are saying to yourself, "I can't. It is too late now. I am too old, and I don't know the right people"—in other words, if you are mentally feeding on all the reasons why you cannot do something or be what you want to be—you are not making "thy flock to rest at noon."

At *noon* the sun casts no shadow; likewise, when you pray, you are not to permit any shadow of fear or doubt to cross your path or deflect you from your goal or aim in life. The world of confusion shall be rejected and you shall mentally partake of, or meditate on, the reality of your desire.

"Behold, thou art fair, my love; behold, thou art fair; thou hast doves' eyes." The *dove* is a symbol of God's inner peace.

I once talked with an alcoholic who said, "Don't say anything about this God-stuff to me. I don't want God. I want a healing." This man was deeply resentful toward a former wife who had remarried; moreover, he was full of grudges against several other people. He needed the *doves' eyes,* which means he needed to see the truth that would give him peace of mind.

I asked him, "Will you pray with me now? All I ask is that you be sincere; if you are, you will experience an inner peace which passeth all human understanding."

He then relaxed his body, and I_ said to him, "Imagine you are talking to the Invisible Presence within you—the Almighty Power which created the Cosmos. It can do all things. Say, 'Thank you, thank you, for this inner peace.' Say it over and over again."

After ten minutes in silent meditation, he was blinded by an interior, Inner Light. It seemed to come from the floor near where he was. The whole room was flooded with Light!

He exclaimed, "All I see is Light! What's wrong?" Then he relaxed into sleep in my office, and his face seemed illumined. He awakened in about fifteen minutes and was completely at peace, saying, "God truly is! God is!" This man had found his beloved, i.e. his sense of oneness with God and all things Good.

As you fall asleep at night, tell your desire how fair it is and how wonderful you would feel in realizing it. Begin to fall in love with your ideal. Praise it; exalt it. "Arise, my Love!" Feel that you are what you want to be. Go to sleep in the consciousness of being or doing what you long to do.

I once told a man on one of the islands where I was visiting to "sleep" on the idea of success. He was selling magazine subscriptions. He became a great success by following this procedure: I suggested that he think of success prior to sleep, i.e. what success meant to him; what he would do if he were successful. I told him to use his imagination; then, as he was about to go to sleep, to fall in love with the idea of success in this way: Repeat the one word "success" over and over again. He should get into the mood of success, then drop off to sleep in the arms of his Everlasting Lover, i.e. his Divine Presence, which would bring to pass whatever he accepted as true. The conditions, experiences, and events of your life are called children of your mind.

"He brought me to the banqueting house, and his banner over me was love." The *banquet house* is your own mind where you entertain the idea or desire of your heart.

I will illustrate at this point how to entertain in this *banquet house* of your own mind. A young girl with a special talent for singing was having great difficulty getting anything to do in the motion picture field, television, or radio. She had been turned down so often she feared she was getting a rejection complex. However, she heard me state over one of our radio programs that whatever the mind of man could imagine and feel as true, he could realize. She wrote that down, came to one of our classes, and began to practice entering into the *banquet house* by quieting the wheels of her mind and relaxing the body by simply talking to it and telling it to relax; it has to obey you. In that quiet, relaxed, peaceful state, with her attention completely focused on an imaginary movie contract in her hand, she felt the reality of the joy and wonder of it all. She was now in the *banquet house,* and the *banner* over her was *love. Love* is an emotional attachment. She was definitely mentally attached to this contract . . . *and calleth those things which be not as though they were* (Romans 4:17). The visible world comes out of the invisible. She caused the contract to become a reality by becoming emotionally attached to the imaginary picture of a contract in her mental *banquet house.* She knew that what she imagined and believed to be so must come to pass in the three-dimensional world.

"His left hand is under my head, and his right hand doth embrace me." The *left hand* is your deep, subjective feeling; the *right hand* is your disciplined imagination. As you begin to imagine and feel the reality of your desire, you are joining the right and left hands together in a Divine embrace; then a union of the idea and feeling takes place. Another way of saying this is: There is an agreement of the conscious and subconscious mind which denotes the answered prayer.

You know that when there is no longer any argument or doubt in your conscious or subconscious mind, your prayer is answered, because the two have agreed as touching upon it, and it is so.

"My beloved spake, and said unto me, Rise up, my love, my fair one, and come away." Is not that what your goal, aim, ambition, or desire is saying to you? For instance, the idea of perfect health is now beckoning to you and saying, "Rise up and come away from the belief in sickness, limitation, pain, and aches to health, harmony, and peace of mind."

I had a long talk with a man in England who had trouble with his leg. He had been confined to his home for nine months and was unable to lean on his leg or walk. The first thing I did was to ask him what he would do if he were healed. He said, "I would again play polo, swim, golf, and climb the Alps, which I used to do every year." That was the answer I was seeking.

I told him in the simplest way how to achieve the perfect use of his legs again. The first thing was to imagine he was actually doing the things he would do. I painted an imaginary picture for him. For fifteen or twenty minutes, three times each day, he sat in his study and imagined he was playing polo; he assumed the mental mood of actually performing the role of a polo player. He became the actor; an actor participates in the role.

Note carefully that he did not see himself playing polo, that would be an illusion. He *felt* himself playing polo. He actualized it by living the drama in his mind or *banquet house.*

At noon he would quiet the mind, still the body, and feel his Alpine clothes on him. He would feel and imagine he was climbing the Alps; he would feel the cold air on his face and hear the voices of his old associates. He lived the drama and felt the naturalness and the tangibility of the rocks.

At night prior to sleep, before going into the Arms of his Beloved— His Deeper Self—he would play a game of golf. He would hold the club, touch the ball with his hand, put it in place, and tee off. He would swing his clubs and delight in watching where the ball went.

When he was in the mood of playing a good game, he would relax in a deep and healthful sleep, feeling very satisfied and happy about his experience.

Within two months this man's leg was healed, and he did all the things he imagined he would do. The *idea* of climbing the Alps, plus the *desire* to play polo again, meant to this man, "Arise, my love, my fair one, and come away" from your belief in a physical handicap. That is what he did.

The law of the subconscious is one of compulsion. When you subjectively feel you are swimming—for example, when you feel the chill of the water and the naturalness of your various swimming strokes—you will sooner or later be compelled to swim. Whatever the handicap, whether fear or a physical condition, you will do what you subjectively felt you were doing.

Your desire, dream, ambition, goal, or aim is your saviour! It is walking down the corridor of your mind, saying to you, "Arise, my love, and come away" and enjoy the good and glorious things of life.

No matter what the problem is or its magnitude, you have really nothing to do but convince yourself of the truth which you are affirming. As quickly as you succeed in convincing yourself of the reality of your desire, results will automatically follow. Your subconscious mind will faithfully reproduce what you impregnated it with.

The Bible says, *Choose you this day whom ye will serve* (Joshua 24:15). You have the freedom to choose the tone, feeling, or mood you enter into. The manifestation of your feeling or conviction is the secret of your lover or subconscious mind. Your external actions are, therefore, determined by your subconscious beliefs and impressions.

Your thought and feeling determine your destiny. The knowledge of the truth is saying to you now, "The winter is past, the rain is over and gone." The *winter* represents that cold state when the seeds are frozen in the bosom of the earth and nothing is growing. The winter and all the seasons are in your mind.

Are your desires, dreams, visions, and aims in life frozen within you because of fear, worry, or false beliefs? You can resurrect them now by turning away from appearances, and enter into the *banquet house* of God within you, saying to yourself, "I can be what I want to be. All I have to do is to impress my subconscious mind with my desire for health, wealth, companionship, or true place, and it will express that state with which I have impressed it."

The *winter* is now over for you; the *rain* is gone, also. Your mind may have been flooded with negative thoughts, causing the mood of despondency, dejection, and melancholia. This is what a flood or avalanche of negative thoughts, false beliefs, and erroneous opinions will do. Now you know that all you have to do is to fill your mind with the truths of God which have come down to you from time immemorial. As you do this, you will crowd out of your mind everything unlike them.

The winter and the floods are over for you when regularly and systematically you fill your mind with the concepts of peace, happiness, love, and goodwill. You can do this by reading one of the Psalms, such as the Twenty-third or the Ninety-first, feeling the truth of everything you say; or you can read aloud a good meditation of the real truths of God. (See, for example, the author's *Special Meditations for Health, Wealth, Love, and Expression* and *Quiet Moments with God*, both published by DeVorss & Company.) As you do this, these truths go in through the eye and the ear; they release a tremendous, therapeutic vibration which courses through your entire mind and body. These curative, healing, soothing vibrations destroy, neutralize, and obliterate all the negative, fearful, diseased thoughts which caused all the trouble in your life; their embodiment must then disappear. This is prayer; do it often enough until it becomes a habit. Prayer should be a habit.

Do everything from the standpoint of the One God and His Love. For instance, when you shop, pray before purchasing. Say, "God guides me in all my purchases." Say quietly to the saleslady or salesman, "God is prospering you."

Whatever you do, do it with love and goodwill. Pour out love, peace, and goodwill to all. Claim frequently that God's Love and Transcendent Beauty flow through all your thoughts, words, and actions. Make a habit of this. Fill your mind with the eternal verities; then you will see that "The flowers appear on the earth; the time of the singing of birds is come"! You begin to *flower*; yes, you will begin to blossom forth.

The *earth* means your body, environment., social life, and all things necessary on this objective plane.

The *flowers* you witness will be the birth of God in your mind. The *flowers* of God's Guidance will watch over you and lead you to green pastures and still waters. The flowers of God's Love will fill your heart. Now, instead of seeing discord anywhere, you will see the Love of God operating in all His Creation; as you realize It, you will see love come forth and flower in the other.

When you go into a home and you see confusion, quarreling, and strife, you will realize within yourself that the peace of God reigns supreme in the minds and hearts of all those in this house; you will see the flower of peace made manifest and expressed.

When you see financial lack and limitation, you will realize the infinite abundance and wealth of God forever flowing, filling up all the empty vessels and leaving a Divine surplus. As you do this, you will live in the garden of God where only orchids and similar flowers of great beauty grow; for only God's ideas circulate in your mind.

As you go to sleep every night, you will clothe yourself with the garment of love, peace, and joy. From now on you always go to sleep feeling that you now are what you long to be. Your last concept as you fall asleep is etched on your deeper mind; you shall resurrect it. Always take into the *banquet house* of your lover (subconscious mind) a noble, God-like concept of yourself; your lover (subconscious mind) will always give you what you conceive and believe as true. Anything you can conceive, you can achieve. Love gives birth to all things. Your tomorrows are determined by your concept of yourself as you fall asleep in the arms of your lover (your ideal).

The time of the singing of birds is at hand for you when you cease singing that old song of lack. You have listened to people sing this kind of song; it is like an old phonograph record: "I'm so lonesome; things never went right for me. I never had a chance. I have been cruelly treated." "I have been operated on three times." "You should hear about all the money I lost." Yes, then they tell about the fear on the lonely road, plus their likes, dislikes, pet peeves, and hates. Imbued with God's love, you will no longer sing that song again. You will sing the new song; for God's ideas and truths *(birds)* will sing in you.

Then you will speak in a new tongue, which means the mood of peace, joy, goodwill, and love. You will no longer react to people and conditions as you formerly did. The Song of God is now heard. Now when someone says something mean or nasty to you, you will immediately transform it by realizing that God's peace fills your soul. You will consume it with the fire of right thoughts; the birds will truly sing in your mind and heart as you do. You are happy; you are bubbling over with enthusiasm, and you are looking forward with a joyous expectancy to all good things. Wherever you go, you carry peace with you; all those who come within your orbit are blessed by your inner radiance. You begin to see sermons in stones, tongues in trees, songs in running brooks, and God in everything. *The voice of the turtledove* is now heard in your land!

Tennyson said, "Speak to Him thou, for He hears, spirit with spirit shall meet, closer is He than breathing, and nearer than hands and feet."

The voice of the turtledove is the voice of peace, the voice of intuition and of God's inner Guidance. You can hear it by lowly listening. For instance, one time as a boy I was lost in the woods. I sat down under a tree and remembered a prayer which starts with, "Our Father, He will show us the way; let us be quiet, and He will lead us." I quietly repeated, "Father, lead us."

90

A wave of peace came over me which I can still recall. *The voice of the turtledove* became real. The *turtledove* is intuition, which means being taught from within. An overpowering feeling came over me to go in a certain direction as if I were being pushed ahead. Two of the boys came with me; the others did not. We were led out of that thick jungle as if by an Unseen Hand.

Great musicians have listened and heard the music within; they wrote down what they heard inwardly. In meditation Lincoln listened to the principle of liberty; Beethoven heard the principle of harmony.

If you are intensely interested in the science of mathematics, you are loving it; as you love it, it will reveal all its secrets to you.

Jesus heard the voice of the turtledove when he said, Peace I leave with you; my peace I give unto you; not as the world giveth, give I unto you. Let not your heart be troubled; neither let it be afraid (John 14:27). How wonderful you will feel as you drink in these words and fill your mind with their therapeutic potency!

Job heard the voice of the turtledove when he said, Acquaint now thyself with Him, and be at peace (job 22:21). Thou wilt keep him in perfect peace, whose mind is stayed on thee: because he trusteth in thee (Isaiah 26:3). For God is not the author of confusion, but of peace (1 Corinthians 14:33).

You can hear *the voice of the turtledove* by turning to the Infinite Intelligence within you, saying, "Father, this is what I want . . . "; then state specifically and clearly the thing you desire. You are now turning your desire over to the God-Wisdom within you, which knows all, sees all, and has the "know-how" of accomplishment. You always know whether you have really turned your request over or not. If you are at peace about it, you have turned it over. If you are anxious and worried, you have not subjectified your prayer; you do not fully trust the God-Wisdom within.

If you want guidance, claim that Infinite Intelligence is guiding you now; It will differentiate Itself as right action for you.

91

You will know you have received the answer, for the dove of peace will whisper in your ear, "Peace, be still." You will know the Divine answer, for you will be at peace, and your decision will be right.

A girl was wondering recently whether to accept a position in New York for considerably more money or remain in Los Angeles in her present position. At night as she went to sleep, she asked herself this question: "What would be my reaction if I had made the right decision now?" The answer came to her, "I would feel wonderful. I would feel happy having made the right decision," and she began to say, "Isn't it wonderful! Isn't it wonderful!" over and over again, as a lullaby, and lulled herself to sleep in the feeling, "It is wonderful."

She had a dream that night, and the voice in the dream said, "Stand still! Stand still!" She awakened immediately and knew of course that this was *the voice of the turtledove—the* voice of intuition

The fourth-dimensional self within her can see ahead, it knows all and sees all, it can read the minds of the owners of the

business in New York. She remained in her present position. Subsequent events proved the truth of her Inner Voice, the eastern concern went into bankruptcy. *I the Lord will make myself known unto him in a vision, and will speak unto him in a dream* (Numbers 12:6).

"My beloved is mine, and I am his, he feedeth among the lilies." The *lilies* represent the poppies which grow in the East. To see the poppy field sway in the breeze is a very beautiful sight. Here the inspired biblical writer is telling you to have a romance with God-like qualities in your mind. As you turn to the God-Presence, It turns to you. You experience the mystic marriage, the wedded bliss, when you fall madly in love with truth for truth's sake, then you become full of the new wine, the new interpretation of life.

The *lilies* symbolize beauty, order, symmetry, and proportion. As you feed or feast on the great truth that God is Indescribable Beauty, Boundless Love, Absolute Bliss, Absolute Harmony, and Infinite Peace, you are truly *feeding among the lilies.* When you claim that what is true of God is true of you, miracles will happen in your life.

By realizing and knowing that these qualities and attributes of God are being expressed through you and that you are a channel for the Divine, every atom of your being begins to dance to the rhythm of the Eternal God. Beauty, order, harmony, and peace appear in your mind, body, and business world as you *feed among the lilies*; you feel your oneness with God, Life, and God's Infinite Riches. You are married to your Beloved, for you are now married to your ideal or desire; you are a bride of the Lord—your dominant conviction. From this moment forward you will bring forth children of your Beloved; they will bear the image and likeness of your idea and feeling.

The father is God's idea; the mother is the emotionalizing of the idea, and its subjective embodiment. From that union of idea and feeling comes forth your health, abundance, happiness, and inner peace.

Sit down and *feed among the lilies* by realizing that every night of the year when you go to sleep, you go before the King of Kings, the Lord of Lords, and the Prince of Peace. Be sure you are "dressed properly" as you enter into the Divine Presence. If you were going before the President, you would put on your best clothes. The clothes you wear as you enter into the heavens of your own mind every night represent the mood, or the tone you wear. Be sure it is always the wedding garment of love, peace, and goodwill to all.

Be absolutely sure that you can say, "Behold, thou art fair." There must be no resentment, ill-will, condemnation of self or others, and no criticism of any person. God's Love must really fill your heart for all men everywhere. You must sincerely wish for everyone what you wish for yourself; then you can say to your mood or feeling, "Behold, thou art fair." *And when ye stand praying, forgive, if ye have ought against any* (Mark 11:25).

"My beloved is mine." All that God is, is yours, for God is within you. All you can possibly desire is already yours. You need no help from the outside to *feed among the lilies*.

When you go to sleep tonight, forgive everyone, and imagine and feel that your desire is fulfilled. Become absolutely and completely indifferent to all thought of failure, because you now know the law. As you accept the end, you have, as Troward so beautifully stated, "willed the means to the realization of the end." As you are about to enter sleep, galvanize yourself into the feeling of being or having your desire. Your mental acceptance of your desire as you go to sleep is your oneness with your Beloved; then this is your conviction in the subconscious mind which gives you that which you impressed upon it.

He feedeth among the lilies. Until the day break, and the shadows flee away. The *shadows* are fear, doubt, worry, anxiety, and all the reasons why you cannot do something. The *shadows* of our five senses and the race belief hover over the minds of all as we pray.

When you pray, accept as true what your reason and five senses deny and reject. Remain faithful to your idea by being full of faith every step of the way. When your consciousness is fully qualified with the acceptance of your desire, all the fear will go away. Trust in the reality of your ideal or desire until you are filled full of the feeling of being it; then you will experience the joy of the answered prayer. Yes, the answer to your prayer will come and light up the heavens of your mind, bringing you peace.

No matter what the problem is, nor how acute, dark, or hopeless things seem to be, turn now to God and say, "How is it in God and Heaven?" The answer will softly steal over your mind like the dew from heaven: "All is peace, joy, bliss, perfection, wholeness, harmony, and beauty." Then reject the evidence of your senses, and *feed among the lilies* of God and Heaven, such as peace, harmony, joy, and perfection. Realize that what is true of God also must be true of you and your surroundings. Continue in this abiding trust and faith in God *until the day break and the shadows flee away.*

Made in the USA
Middletown, DE
23 November 2020